A HARVEST OF SUNFLOWERS

By the same author from Allison & Busby Ltd

A House in the Sunflowers

A Harvest of Sunflowers

RUTH SILVESTRE

Illustrated by Michael Grater

This edition first published in Great Britain in 1997 by
Allison & Busby Limited
Suite 111, Bon Marche Centre
241-251 Ferndale Road
London SW9 8BJ
http://www.allisonandbusby.ltd.uk

Copyright © 1996 by Ruth Silvestre
Illustrations copyright © 1996 by Michael Grater

Reprinted 2001

The right of Ruth Silvestre to be identified as
author of this work has been asserted by her in
accordance with the Copyright, Designs and
Patents Act, 1988

A catalogue record for this book is available from
the British Library.

ISBN 0 7490 0417 7

Printed and bound in Spain by
Liberduplex, s.l. Barcelona.

for David

Acknowledgements

Thanks to Simone Larive and Tony White

1

It is hard to believe that this will be our twentieth summer at Bel-Air, our house in the sunflowers. The details of that first glimpse on a hot and hazy day are still vivid. We had been searching intermittently for three years and were leaving England at the end of the week. As we followed the sun-burned, bare-legged farmer on his small motorcycle up through the maize, head high on either side of the bumpy track, we had no idea what we would find. M. Bertrand, his chin still greasy from eating *confit de canard*, was reluctantly interrupting his midday meal to show us the house he had for sale. Our thirteen-year-old son Matthew leaned out of the camper window as we approached what appeared to be a complete ruin. Turning to look back at us, the farmer shook his head, his *mobylette* wobbled and we breathed again. We turned right, passing a dried-up pond, a barn wall and turning again, stopped in front of an old stone house with a long sloping roof and a well under the wide porch. The broken shutters were closed. We looked at it in a silence broken only by the sound of crickets. It seemed to be asleep. It was not a ruin but, had it been left empty another twelve years, would have certainly become one. The tiles were haphazard, sliding down the roof. Inside there was a stream of green lichen across the wall of the main room, and all the wooden floors were eaten away. But there was also something else; a spirit of place. This house had once been loved and cared for, and it has been our project, our joy and our delight, ever since that day.

In these twenty years we have come to realise how very fortunate we were to find both this particular house and the friendship of M. and Madame Bertrand, who, very quickly, became Raymond and Claudette. Together we have watched our children grow up. Their son and daughter and our two sons, who are now beginning their own families. We have also looked back and learned a little of the people who lived at Bel-Air before us. Anaïs Costes came as a young bride in 1889 and lived here until she died in 1961. Her only son Aloïs was crippled with polio as a boy. He never married. When she died he could not manage without her and died five years later. Her husband Justin, as the eldest of the three brothers born at Bel-air, inherited the property. Justin died of a heart attack when he was only fifty-two, leaving Anaïs and her handicapped son to look after everything.

Those who remember her always say, '*Ah oui, Anaïs... elle était vaillante.*' Two photographs of her hang on my wall. One when she was in her twenties with her young son at her side holding a hoop, and another taken much later at a family wedding. She was then sixty-two. Her face is lined but her smile is almost mischievous. She wears a brooch to pin her collar and a plain head band. Her son looks very smart in a stiff collar, his hair neatly arranged. I have faded photographs of her husband and brother-in-law, taken during their periods of compulsory military service when they were young. They are handsome and carefree in their uniforms. Now we are hanging our own dynasty on the opposite side of the wall, photographs of our children and grandchildren, who will be the next guardians of Bel-Air.

This is the short holiday, the flying visit. Not that we fly any more – Eurostar has changed all that. After London to Paris, the TGV takes us to Agen – pronounced Agenne by the people who live there – and if we travel on a Friday, there is a good connection to Monsempron Libos. We are told that it is a station that SNCF would dearly love to close but, so far, petitions to retain its services have succeeded. The station house is painted a deep yellow ochre, its white edging and shuttered upper windows giving it a residential look. Shaded by a Mediterranean cypress, doves sit cooing from the painted corbels. Sometimes we take the night train direct from Paris which arrives here just after six in the morning. If it happens to be a Thursday, the first traders will be unrolling their umbrellas to set up the weekly market, the largest in the region, when the whole town is closed to traffic.

We are in Lot-et-Garonne, six hundred miles south of Calais, and it shows. Most of the people who come in from miles around both to buy and sell are short and dark, with wide faces and ready smiles. The local accent is strong, with rolled r's, and the last syllables pronounced emphatically. If it is summer the stalls will be piled high with melons and nectarines, strawberries and peaches, artichokes, the finest french beans and twenty kinds of olives. There will be the squeal of piglets and the smells of paella cooking in a giant pan, quails roasting on a spit, goat cheese and strings of garlic.

Whatever time we arrive we know our friends will meet us. We hug each other and stand back to look. Perhaps a little thinner or, more likely, fatter; always, alas, a little older.

This time it is Claudette who has come to collect us. We hurry home along the familiar roads.

'I see they've had a new roof at Mathilde's old house.'

'Yes, just before Christmas.'

'Ah, M. Lombard is still planting sunflowers in his top field then. Good.'

'Would you like a drink before you go up?'

As we climb out of the car, Claudette's elderly parents, Granny and Grandpa, stick in hand, come very slowly across the courtyard from different directions, like two old snails. Grandpa has used a stick for many years but it is the first time for Grandma. Her back is noticeably more crooked but her face is plump and rosy and her smile as sweet as ever.

'*Ça va, Mami?*'

She shrugs. '*Tout doucement*' ... slowly.

Grandpa shakes our hands peering up uncertainly, then suddenly smiles and nods.

'Eh! Oh!' shouts Claudette across the courtyard. From the nearest orchard, through the gate by the first barn where the chickens scurry out of his way, Raymond comes to greet us. He kisses me warmly and beams.

'*Ça va?*'

'*Oh, pas trop.*'

'Why? What's the matter?'

'It's my shoulder. I can't remember what I was doing. I turned my arm and ... *clac!*' He stops himself just in time from repeating the movement, so eager is he to explain. He's had an X-ray but it showed nothing. It's a ligament. He's had physiotherapy, acupuncture – nothing helps.

'Rest?' I suggest. He laughs.

We troop up into the familiar kitchen. Cats are tipped off chairs and we sit. On the shelf there is a large, gaudy trophy which Raymond displays with pride. Once again they have won the prize at the special '*soirée de dégustations, de convivialité et d'humeur*', which is given each Autumn by the local *Cave Coopérative*. It was apparently a great evening. There were two hundred participants Raymond tells us, his

4

eyes shining. Each *producteur* competes to encourage the greatest sale of wine from the *Cave*, and Raymond's success is due in no small measure to all our friends and family who put every purchase down on his total. In addition to the cup he is also rewarded with his own weight in wine. We shall not go thirsty this holiday.

'*A la vôtre!*'

'*A la tienne Étienne!*'

'No problems up at the house?'

Raymond shakes his head. 'And your 2CV is working. I started it this morning.'

Claudette drives us up the track, past the farm in which their daughter Véronique now lives with her husband and three-year-old child, and we see Bel-Air for the first time for eight months. There are swathes of wild marguerites interspersed with love-in-a-mist just waiting to bloom. The wisteria is past its best but the *boule-de-neige* is heavy with round white blossom. The valerian which I planted two years ago, has at last taken off and the mallow bushes are as abundant as heavily pregnant girls. Will they flower before we have to leave?

The porch is a blaze of colour. Claudette has planted all the pots along the wall with petunias, marigolds, busy lizzies and small dianthus.

'Oh, how lovely!'

Pleased that I have noticed, she briskly dead-heads a geranium.

'*Alors ... à ce soir ... vers huit heures.*' And she's gone.

There are eggs and walnuts and wine on the working surface. There are more flowers in a jug on the table, lilac, arum lilies, roses and white irises, and four very tired looking apples in a bowl. But they are all '*fabrication maison*'.

We make the bed, unpack and then tour the garden to see what else has survived. We look at the weeds and the long grass which Raymond has roughly cut. There is so much to do – but we have two weeks. The air is sweet and clean, blowing gently from the south-west. We can see down across *le grand champ*, as Raymond always calls it. It is newly sewn with maize and the thin green lines give it an odd perspective. They are never completely straight but curve gently and in the corners there are strips of cross-hatching where the great machine made a few extra turns.

In the meadow at the far edge of the field a herd of pale cows – *les Blondes d'Aquitaine* – move slowly, and beyond the pasture is a band of woodland with a central gap through which we can see the farm. There are four buildings side by side, all built at different times. The earliest part is marked on the map of 1765. The church spire from which the angelus rings three times a day rises above the trees. Seven in the morning, midday, and seven in the evening – the only hours a farmer really needs to know.

Beyond the village the ground rises again. The skyline is scalloped with the rolling banks on the far side of the river Lot. It is a gentle landscape. A car passes silently on the road below. Unless it is a very heavy lorry it does not disturb the peace. The only sounds are the drone of a distant tractor and the call of hens. From the front of the house we look up past a meadow where more cows will soon be brought to graze after the hay is cut. Beyond that is the new vineyard and then another wood which stretches up to the highest point for miles around, where the *château d'eau* – the water tower – nestles into the hillside. There was mains water already here when we bought the house but no tap. Anaïs and her son were too poor, or too frugal, to pay for water. They preferred to rely on the well under the porch and the pond at the end of the track.

To the west there is more gently rolling hillside and a wood which curves. Who cut that shape I wonder? One thinks of this landscape as timeless but I now know that the ruin at the end of the track was once a large house. Aloïs, so I'm told, used to do odd jobs for the family who lived there.

They are always referred to as *'les Carles'*. For some reason they decided to move. They demolished much of their property and, putting the stones on carts, moved down into the village and built two small houses. There are always changes. Even the track which now goes past the back of our house, once passed the front door, and recently we were surprised to learn that there was once a church, Saint Nicholas, now completely vanished, just across the next field. These seemingly solid buildings with their metre thick walls were cemented with earth and, once the roof goes, the rain eventually washes them away.

The smaller creatures here are adept at renewing their shelters. The miner bees, who live in ever greater numbers on my south-facing terrace, patiently re-excavate their neat cylindrical holes when a sweep of the broom upsets them. The tunnel spiders patch and weave when their intricate webs are broken and the ants rush in concerted effort to rebury their eggs in the disturbed anthill. There is the time and quiet here in which to wind down and observe this other world. As I rested briefly from weeding, an ant dragging a dead grub three times its own size caught my eye. As it passed beneath my chair I turned to watch it. Such a cumbersome burden was not easy to manipulate. On and on it went, over small stones, up grass stems and down again, the grub tipping perilously from one side to the other. Occasionally the ant abandoned it altogether and turned a small rapid circle as if to get its bearings – then off it went again, dragging the long, fast dying corpse. I moved my chair some three metres ahead. The ant soon passed me and I moved again. Its energy and speed at close quarters was amazing. It arrived at a hole in the stone wall. Home at last? No. On it went another three metres, to disappear in the undergrowth at the end of the terrace. I decided to try to find the nest. The first pile of earth was an old molehill, also the second. I had to walk to the very edge of our land before I found it. I set down my chair and waited. Would the ant get eaten by some other predator as it penetrated the great green forest of cow parsley – or, almost worse, would its booty be stolen? I watched other ants scurrying back and forth – some bringing home a small fly but nothing as spectacular as my ant's giant burden. Just as I began to think I had lost it altogether out it came – the juggernaut trailing its great load. On and on across the rough grass littered now with scraps of pampas leaf, it reached the edge of the nest. This last stretch was the hardest; there were no easy, ground floor entrances. I watched as it hauled its trophy up the steep incline to the very top. I blinked and it had gone. Such are the distractions from gardening – and from writing.

When we first bought Bel-Air there was so much work to be done on the house that writing about it was the last thing on my mind. Even later, when I had had an article published, I never contemplated a book. It is now eight years since I wrote the first book and so many things have changed as they must do in all lives. We are still working on the house, still making plans for both inside and out. We are very conscious that we have had the great fortune, both to be able to share our summers with good friends and neighbours and, on that hot and hazy day, to have found Bel-Air.

2

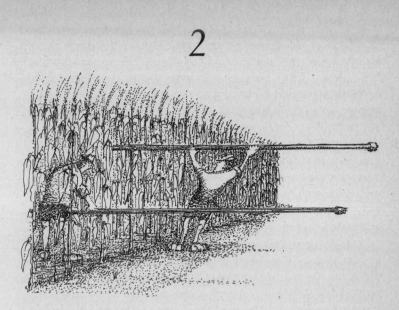

It was on the 14th of July 1989, the two hundredth anniversary of the storming of the Bastille, that I signed the
contract for *A House in the Sunflowers,* my first book about
our house in south-west France, but the manuscript might
well never have been finished if I had not developed acute
sciatica in the spring of that year. I had had the odd
problem with my back for several years. I suspect that
lifting heavy stones to make our first terrace at Bel-Air was
the original cause, but a visit to the physiotherapist, a
painkiller or two and a few days rest had always done the
trick. Not this time. Unable to walk more than half a dozen
steps I tried various remedies but, as May turned into June,
the improvement was imperceptible. How I longed to go to
France, but what could I do if I got there? And there was
always the chance that the next treatment might find a cure.
If I couldn't make my usual spring visit, at least I could
write about it. If it never got into print it would be a family
record. Immobile in my study in Clapham I wished myself

across the Channel and the great plains of northern France, across the Loire and the Dordogne to the peace of our other home overlooking the valley of the river Lot. By the end of June the manuscript was finished and sent off to my agent.

A few days later Clive Allison of Allison and Busby rang me to say how much he had enjoyed reading it and that he would like to publish it the following spring. Surprised and delighted, I felt that at least something had been achieved through all those hours of sitting still and signing the contract on the 14th of July seemed a good omen. But I was to learn much about what was to me, this new world of publishing. Within weeks, Clive Allison had been replaced by Peter Day who fortunately, seemed equally enthusiastic. He wanted some photographs of Bel-Air, as many as possible. Exactly the spur I needed; sciatica or not, I determined to go. As we made our preparations I realised how many steps there were between wardrobe and suitcase. Last-minute shopping was out of the question as was our usual summer three-day sight-seeing journey down through France.

'We'll put the car on the train as far as Brive,' said my ever solicitous husband. 'Then we'll be there well before the 29th of July.'

This was the day I had been desperate not to miss. Philippe – Raymond and Claudette's son, who had been a brown, skinny thirteen year old when we first met him – was to be married to the most beautiful girl in the next village. I lay on my bunk on the journey from Boulogne to Brive, in the Dordogne, regretting all the places we were whizzing through while Mike, more sensibly, enjoyed the passing kilometres that he didn't have to drive. As dawn broke we joined the sleepy-eyed who stumbled from the train and I had to breakfast from a convenient luggage trolley as the splendid new dining room was too far down the platform for me to reach.

What a joy to drive out into the French countryside as the sun appeared. It seemed so long since we had last come.

I feasted my eyes as the steeper roofs of the Périgord flattened out into those of the south, and brilliant fields of sunflowers told me that we were nearing home. But the irrigation lakes were low, the grass verges like pale straw, and I wondered about my garden.

At last we climbed the dusty track to Bel-Air. The parched fields shimmered on either side and Raymond's plum trees seemed to crackle in the heat. The garden was, as I had feared, like a desert. Everything was desperate for water, even the plants on the porch which Claudette usually tended. The shutters had been opened for our arrival and there were flowers and wine on the table but, as I hobbled from room to room, it became clear that Claudette's usual brisk sweep through had not happened. Of course – the wedding! She would have been trying to get everything done on the farm to leave the following week clear. I was lucky to have the house opened up at all.

'*C'est le mariage!*' She smiled apologetically as she welcomed us down to supper as she always does on our first evening. I climbed carefully from the car and moved slowly across the courtyard. Raymond's jaw dropped.

'*Mais* ... what's the matter with you?' he demanded.

'*La sciatique,*' I replied.

He threw up his hands. '*Oh malheur!*' he cried, and I reckoned that just about said it.

Grandma and Grandpa, both over eighty, came to greet us as if almost surprised at their survival of another winter and it was wonderful to sit down together once more and ladle out Claudette's vegetable soup. Slices of her *pâté de porc* were followed by a savoury rice pudding, made with milk, but containing sliced courgettes and scraps of ham and with a topping of breadcrumbs and cheese. Next came a dish of roast chicken with sautéed potatoes and a green salad. We were still catching up with all the local news as we ate a great dish of strawberries, then handed round the coffee while Claudette fetched the obligatory jar of prunes *à l'eau de vie*.

Raymond looked at me with concern. 'Have you been to a doctor?' he asked.

'Too many,' I sighed, recalling the useless cortisone injections, the massage, the acupuncture, and all the manipulations.

'You should try *la guérisseuse*,' he urged.

'*La guérisseuse*?'

'*Oui, Madame Orlando.*'

'What does she do?'

'She just touches you. *Elle a le don.*' The gift. Madame Orlando, it seemed, was a faith healer.

'She's very good,' encouraged Raymond.

Grandpa nodded. '*C'est vrai*,' he shouted.

'*Ça depend*,' said Grandma. 'She didn't do much for my back ...'

'Oh,' Grandpa shrugged. 'At your age ...'

'She's not as good as old Léon,' insisted Grandma.

Another healer? *Les guérisseurs* it seemed, were commonplace.

Claudette spooned the prunes into our still warm coffee cups. 'Yes, it was old Léon that cured Marianne ... You know ... Roland's daughter.'

I was surprised. Roland, Claudette's second cousin, is a teacher of gymnastics and not, I would have thought, someone to trust his daughter to a faith healer.

'What was the matter with Marianne?' I asked.

'*Elle avait un zona*,' said Claudette.

'It took him over half an hour,' said Raymond. 'But all she had afterwards was a small round mark on her chest and no pain at all.'

A search in the dictionary told us that Marianne had been cured of shingles, but as it appeared that old Leon had since died, he wasn't going to be much help to me.

'Mind you, he was a strange old man. He treated you in his dirty garage,' said Claudette, wrinkling her nose. 'And he never wore anything on his feet but his old slippers.'

Madame Orlando, it seemed, was more *à la mode*.

'*Une belle femme*,' said Raymond enthusiastically. 'And she can't do you any harm.' This seemed to be the trump card of the faith healer. 'She works from seven in the morning to seven at night – and' he added, his eyes gleaming, '*il faut être en forme pour le mariage!*'

As it was only a week and a half before the great day I rang for *un rendez-vous* the following morning. If Madame Orlando worked a twelve-hour day, she could surely fit me in somewhere. Although I could not walk, driving was, fortunately, not a problem, and I must admit I was curious. I went the next afternoon. Her house was impressive. A picture window looked over a well-watered lawn sloping down to a hedge of conifers. There was a car park sufficient for half a dozen cars and a notice on the door said *SALLE D'ATTENTE ENTREZ*. I obeyed. It was a very hot day, but the lowered blinds made the room cool and shadowy. After about ten minutes, during which time I could hear faint murmurings from a neighbouring room, a door opened. A woman came out carrying a child of about four, clearly paralysed, her head lolling backward. The woman was followed by Madame Orlando herself who stroked the child's cheek, saw them off into the blazing sunshine, then turned to me.

'*Entrez, entrez*,' she said.

'*Une belle femme*' indeed. Almost six feet tall, she wore a brilliant blue shift and her red hair was drawn back from her face in a heavy bun. '*Quelle chaleur!*' she murmured, steaming gently. With her pale skin, as if untouched by the sun, she was like a large and voluptuous magnolia. She led me into her treatment room and sat behind a desk on which were many books, some I noted, on homeopathy. She wasted no time on the taking down of lengthy particulars. She listened as I explained my problem.

'Pull up your shirt,' she said calmly, rubbing her hands together and coming to sit beside me on a stool. For a few seconds she massaged the base of my spine very hard with her thumbs then simply laid one soft, hot hand against my back and, on learning that I was from London, asked if I knew La Didi?

I was puzzled. 'La Didi?'

'*La jolie femme du Prince Charles!*' she enthused in her deep, breathy voice.

On learning that I wasn't exactly an intimate of 'Lady Di' she lost interest in me completely until the fifteen minutes were up and I paid my forty francs in cash.

'Same time next week,' she said, ushering me out past several more incoming patients. It was just as painful to limp to the car but I could still feel the heat from her hand several hours later. Perhaps she might do me good. I was ready to try anything and clearly *la guérisseuse* was very much a part of the local scene. It took me the rest of the week to unpack and sort the house out. It was infuriating to be so inactive. I usually spend the first few days in a positive whirlwind. And as for the garden! Mercifully it rained gently all one night and the following morning I did manage a little weeding, sitting down – a new experience. Not the best, but the only possible, position.

On the farm everyone was preparing for the coming wedding. At the last Sunday lunch with only six days to go everyone sat drinking their aperitifs and waiting for Corinne, the beautiful bride to be.

'Always late!' muttered Grandpa, looking longingly at the soup tureen.

Mike and I hadn't seen her for nearly a year. At that time, although the official fiancée and a frequent visitor, she was always a little hesitant. The fact that she and Philippe had been sharing a flat in Bordeaux was not exactly approved of. There was a sigh of relief as the car turned into the courtyard and a very different Corinne smiled at us all. With a new and glamorous hairstyle she glowed with confidence and excitement. In an elegant red dress she made her entrance with unusual flair, sure of her lines and

14

everyone there! Chattering non-stop she bestowed perfumed kisses all round and, led by an eager Grandpa, we moved to the table and the meal began.

After the soup we ate home cured ham with the first melons of the season and then Claudette served a couscous which was a new venture for her that year.

'Mm, c'est bon, le couscous!' said Corinne, her huge dark eyes sparkling, and we passed round a small jug of sauce made with *harissa* to make it even hotter for those who wished.

'C'est le seul plat,' announced Claudette firmly. Raymond looked up in dismay.

'Aujourd'hui c'est le petit menu. On a trop à faire!' she gave him a look. He made sure he took another helping. After the salad Grandma brought in a plate piled high with *beignets*, the small local doughnut, to be eaten with yet more strawberries. For once it was not recipes, but the details of the wedding that were discussed.

Philippe seemed quietly content and Corinne chatted enough for them both. The latest presents, including the carriage clock which we had brought from London, were opened and approved. She and Véronique, her future sister-in-law, pored over the table plan for the reception. Now, would it be suitable for that aunt to sit next to that cousin? Claudette wasn't sure. Perhaps not. Grandma remembered some past difficulty. Names were rubbed out and others added. Now for the procession. How exactly should she hold her father's arm?

Giggling, they rehearsed, while Grandma and Claudette tried to clear the table. Would the special make-up, which she would have done professionally on the day, hold up to being kissed by – her eyes widened at the thought – at least four hundred and fifty guests? The problems and the excitement were endless.

But even with an imminent wedding, work on the farm had to continue. In spite of a night's rain the ground below the first few inches was rock hard. Water for irrigation was pumped up from a lake dug close to the farm, but every few days Raymond had to change the pipes in the field of maize as they only watered a section at a time. They were long and heavy and it was not really a job for one man. As the maize was already almost head high it was hot and dusty work but vital if the crop was to yield. In dry seasons in the past it had sometimes had to be cut for silage, the cobs not having developed.

While Mike helped Raymond in the broiling sun, I sat in the shade with Claudette and Grandma tying up sugared almonds in circles of white net with satin ribbons.

'How many do we have to do?' I enquired as the pile grew larger.

'About a hundred and fifty,' answered Grandma placidly. 'One for each guest *au repas*. And I suppose we'd better do a few extra,' she added.

The wedding breakfast was not to take place, I learned, until after nine o'clock in the evening.

'*Et le mariage?*'

'Two o'clock at the Marie. Two-thirty at the church,' said Claudette.

'And what happens in between?'

They looked at me in astonishment. 'Why – *le vin d'honneur* of course. A reception for everyone from the two villages.'

'Everyone?'

'Well – I don't suppose everyone will come but there will certainly be over five hundred people.'

With typical French practicality, the two families had already decided to share the cost of what was clearly to be a grand affair. The reception was to be held *chez* Corinne. Her parents were also farmers but, unlike Raymond and Claudette, they specialised in the growing of crops for seed, mostly leeks and carrots. Her mother also kept bees and sold honey.

'They have plenty of land and such a beautiful garden,' said Claudette wistfully. 'Wait till you see. But of course,' she added, 'they have no animals. That makes all the difference.'

'*Ah, les bêtes*,' sighed Grandma. '*Mais ... qu'est que vous voulez?*' She shrugged her thin shoulders and counted out another eight sugared almonds.

Le repas, I was pleased to learn, was to be held at the Restaurant Palissy. The food would certainly be good and we would be looked after by my favourite waiter, the ebullient Monsieur Allo. He had apparently retired from his other job as the local postman, but was as lively as ever.

'And the menu?' I asked.

Claudette laughed '*Oh ... il ne faut pas le dire! C'est un secret.*' But she couldn't resist telling me that one of the courses would be *un rôti de filet de boeuf* which, on the following morning, she would go to choose from her favourite butcher.

'I know the chef at *le Palissy* will cook it to perfection,' she said. 'But I must make sure of the quality. You can't leave anything to chance *pour un mariage*.' *Le vin d'honneur* for the large reception after the ceremony was not in fact to be wine, but a choice between tropical fruit juice and unlimited rum punch. This would be made by Philippe and Corinne's brothers the night before. To eat, there would be the usual nuts and nibbles, quiches and pizzas, and Raymond's niece was providing dozens of hard boiled quail's eggs.

As we finished the last bag of almonds and layered them away in a large carton, Mike and Raymond arrived from the field in the old van. Covered in dust and sweat, they washed briefly under the outside tap, downed a couple of cold beers and disappeared again, the van doors now bulging with a load of chairs and tables. These were to go to Corinne's farm and all the owner's names were written underneath.

The weather grew even hotter. The morning before the wedding there was an urgent telephone call. The father of the bride, who was to have delivered the cases of an '82 Bordeaux, Chateau la Croix to the restaurant that afternoon, had instead to go to hospital for an X-ray. Mending a fence, the farmer's everlasting task, he had apparently been tugging at some barbed wire with heavy pincers, when the wire had snapped and he had hit his nose.

'*Quelle catastrophe!*' said Raymond. 'His nose may well be broken. I shall have to take the wine. It's to go with *le filet*.' His face lit up for a moment with anticipation, then resumed its worried look. 'And there are the trees to go as well, Michel,' he said. 'Do you think we could get them in your car as it's longer and we can open up the back?'

We turned into the long drive which led to Corinne's farm. The garden was as beautiful as Claudette had described it. There were lawns shaded by trees and colourful borders interspersed with dozens of small bushes of lavender and rosemary. But that morning it was a scene of chaos. At least twenty people were running in all directions. Young men were unloading long wooden table tops from a lorry, others were sorting out a mountain of greenery piled outside the house and the father of the bride emerged at that very moment clutching a bloody handkerchief to his nose. His wife, an older, plumper version of her dark-eyed daughter, threw up her hands as she saw us.

'*Mon Dieu!*' she cried, climbing into the car. 'What a time to choose. I have a million things to do.' Then, as if realising that at least a little sympathy was required, she patted his hand and started the engine. 'And imagine,' she shouted as they drove off to the clinic at speed, 'What is he going to look like tomorrow?'

Mike and Raymond loaded the wine into our estate car and Corinne's brothers slid in two tall juniper trees on the top. These were to decorate the doors of the restaurant. They were so long that we had to drive with the rear door tied open and, squeezed in as I had to be, I was not sorry to be dropped off to try my luck once more with the large, hot hand of *la guérisseuse*.

3

The great day dawned. At least it did for Claudette and Véronique, her daughter, who were both at the hairdressers at seven a.m. Knowing that it would be a long day; mercifully not on parade until midday, I didn't get up until eleven. There were some compensations in being *hors de combat*. We wondered how the broken nose was faring.

The sky was cloudless. There was not a breath of wind. As Mike put on his suit and knotted his rarely used tie the temperature rose into the high eighties. I was very glad I had brought an antique silk dress as by mid-afternoon anything synthetic would have been unbearable.

At the farm there was great excitement. Mike's unusually formal appearance was greeted with shouts of approval. Raymond looked as though he had been professionally cleaned and polished, and Claudette emerged triumphantly down the steps wearing a smart little black straw boater and an extravagantly draped dress the exact shade of one of her apricots. Everyone glowed with anticipation. More and more people arrived. The courtyard filled with enthusiastic friends and relations and at one thirty we all moved off to Corinne's farm some three miles away.

On arrival we had to slow to a crawl at the beginning of the long drive as the surface of the road had been decorated with intricate patterns of cut leaves and flowers. What time had they got up to do this we wondered? The courtyard and garden were transformed with tables and chairs arranged under the trees. In the centre a dance-floor had been constructed, arched over with branches of evergreen, wild asparagus fern and dozens of paper roses. We were all directed to a special area behind the great barn, where Corinne's brothers and cousins decorated each car with wild flowers and streamers. Button holes were fixed and everyone was then rehearsed in their positions for the grand procession to the Mairie for the civil ceremony, and afterwards to the church for the blessing.

Corinne's father, his nose happily not broken welcomed everyone. Exquisitely dressed children jumped up and down with excitement as Philippe and Corinne came out onto the garlanded balcony to cheers and whistles. Philippe in a dark suit and wing collar with a pale grey bow tie looked handsome and a little dazed. Corinne was radiant as she walked down the steps in her fairy-tale wedding dress with billowing skirt, a simple spray of flowers in her hair, a worthy leading lady of this whole joyous production. The decorated car aerials glinted in the sunlight. We prepared to move off when suddenly Corinne's mother rushed along the lines of cars.

'Il ne faut pas klaxonner!' she shouted. 'A cause des vaches du voisin!'

It is the custom in France for wedding parties to signal their joyful purpose by sounding their horns almost continuously on their way to and from a wedding. As everything else on this hot afternoon was being done with such enthusiasm Corinne's mother had rightly anticipated a continuous cacophony on leaving. But the message did not get passed along the entire line of cars and the last few, perhaps trying to make up for the unaccustomed silence in front, klaxoned loudly as we left and the neighbour's cows gave us a galloping send-off.

As the civil ceremony in the Mayor's office necessitated standing I was excused. I sat on a wall in the shade and talked to Madame Esther who is well over eighty, on crutches and also not too good at standing. She is the niece of Anaïs, my predecessor at Bel-Air, and I am always glad of a chance to talk to her.

'*Ah, les mariages,*' she sighed. '*Ah oui.* They bring back so many memories.'

And then in her usual fashion she lapsed into a patois so rapid that I was completely lost. But in any case I felt that she was really talking to herself.

The legal part of the wedding over we now processed as rehearsed across the square to the church. More juniper trees graced the porch. On the steps, underneath a garland of paper roses stood the curé to welcome us. Round and kindly, and, at over seventy, officially retired, he has been kept on to serve a community which would otherwise have no priest; as is the case in so many parts of rural France. He beamed at the beautiful young couple and led us all inside into the cool interior until it seemed the church would burst its walls.

It was a strange but moving service, not a traditional nuptial mass. It was a marriage in itself, a mix of the sacred and the secular. A poem *L'amour fragile comme un enfant*, was followed by a fine reading of *The Song of Songs*, which somehow in French sounded especially passionate. As the flash bulbs popped and the video cameras whirled the genial little priest seemed quite content to add the religious content from time to time. When it was all over we poured out of the church into a heat which took our breath away, and Corinne began the kissing for which the make-up had been so specially constructed. But she was so radiant that it was, in any case, unnecessary.

Back once more at the farm the fun, and most importantly, some eating could begin. It was almost four o'clock and the hottest part of the day but no one had had any lunch. Unthinkable! Music from a disco manned by a young relative began and the quails' eggs and pizzas disappeared with speed and were replenished just as quickly. Corinne and her gallant father, his nose just slightly swollen, took to the garlanded dance floor. With a handsome new husband, three brothers and umpteen cousins the bride did not lack for partners. Everyone danced with abandon, even her great aunt, lately retired from religious life. Endless photographs were taken, toasts were proposed, drunk, and proposed again and we processed indoors in smaller groups to view the room full of expensive wedding presents. Granny and Grandpa had bought them a washing machine.

At last the sunlight slanted lower in the sky, the guests who had been invited for *le vin d'honneur* began to leave. The moment came for the one hundred and fifty close friends and family to assemble for the last procession to the so carefully planned wedding meal.

The Restaurant Palissy must have been warned of our imminent arrival by the chorus of 'klaxons' echoing through the valley from Gavaudun. Home of the lepers in the Middle Ages, the caves in which these piteous creatures were forced to live, and from where they lowered their baskets for food can still be seen high up in the cliffs overlooking the idyllic scene below. But our party gave them little thought.

On our arrival juniper trees once more stood sentinel as we filed through the small bar to the large room at the back where M. Allo, a gleaming white napkin over his arm, stood to greet us with his wide anxious smile, and the next six hours passed in a haze of music, wild voices and wonderful food. Again it was a meal to write about. We began with *melon au porto*, followed by salmon braised in champagne. Then the so carefully chosen *rôti de boeuf* with a *sauce Perigueux* was carried in. The sauce was a rich Madeira sauce with the addition of truffles and cognac. It was the best beef I have ever tasted and clearly I was not alone. There were raised eyebrows at the first bite then kissing of fingers, groans of delight and the taking of second helpings as the great platters were passed and repassed. M. Allo, who has been especially solicitous to me since his photograph appeared with an article I had published in *The Lady*, urged me to take a third helping.

'*Mais ... on m'a dit que vous êtes malade,*' he said. '*Il faut bien manger.*'

There was dancing in between the courses, which was just as well, for the beef was followed by roast guinea-fowl cooked with prunes and flambéed in Armagnac, together with potatoes sautéed with garlic, stuffed tomatoes, and green beans. I know there was a salad and a cheese board because I kept the menu but I don't remember eating them. I was watching the dancers. The Lambada was all the rage then and its exotic, pulsating beat was irresistible. Raymond and Claudette spun round the floor as expertly as they always do while Corinne's mother danced with all the young cousins. There was no polite parental decorum but a joyous, uninhibited celebration of life. How I longed to join them on the crowded floor.

Towards midnight more young people began to arrive to fill the dozen or so empty places.

'They've come for *le dessert*,' explained Raymond.

This it seemed was yet another category of guest, invited for the end of the banquet and the dancing. They tucked into enormous helpings of baked alaska washed down with champagne. Corinne came round to everyone with the packets of sugared almonds which I had helped to prepare but there were no speeches. The meal finished with a *pyramide de bonheur*, or *pièce montée*. The French equivalent of a wedding cake, it certainly couldn't be cut up and dispatched in small boxes. It consists of dozens of profiteroles filled with *crème pâtissière* piled high and glued together with stiff caramel to form a small mountain.

Coffee was served, cousins and friends told jokes and did sketches, and the dancing grew wilder. I did manage to sing as requested but had to sit on a stool, something new for me. It felt very odd. It was a wonderful evening, but by half past three I knew sadly that I had had enough. Granny and Grandpa, also tired but not wanting to be the first to leave begged a lift home. 'Aren't you exhausted?' I asked Corinne as I kissed her.

'*Mais non!*' she said. 'Only my feet perhaps.'

I slept nearly all the next day. I was excused the two o'clock Sunday lunch '*en plein air*' chez Corinne, but Mike went and said it was, of course, delicious. Philippe and Corinne had got to bed at five only to be woken at six by a rowdy crowd carrying *le tourin*. This is a custom which is usually performed after *un mariage* but which, as we once discovered in our early days at Bel-Air, can happen at any time anyone feels in the mood. *Le tourin* is a soup fortified with a great deal of garlic which is stealthily brought to the bedside of a sleeping couple by as many people as can cram into the room. It is the signal for yet another party. At last, late on Sunday evening the newly-weds left, not for a honeymoon – that would come two months later – but to prepare for work the following morning. For '*un mariage à la mode du Sud Ouest de la France*' you need to be, as Raymond said '*en forme*' indeed!

4

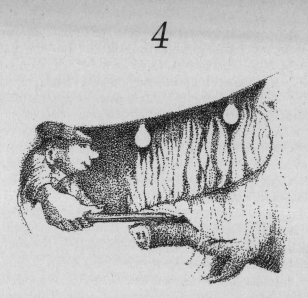

The weather grew hotter. Unable to do very much, and in any case told by everyone that the only cure for sciatica was rest, I unashamedly spent a great deal of that summer just lying around. I found the pain was considerably eased by gently swimming on my back. Our wealthy and generous friends the Thomases who lived about a mile away still kept open pool, complete with champagne. Hugh Fowles, an ex-colleague of Mike's who had bought a nearby ruin and, with his incredible energy, had already restored it, had also made a full-sized pool for his family. It seemed crazy to even dream of a pool of my own, but I began to do so.

One afternoon, following yet another session with the voluptuous *guérisseuse*, the treatment on this occasion having been given to a deafening background of Tom and Jerry capering about on the large screen in the corner of her surgery, I thought a swim might be just as efficacious; certainly quieter. By five o'clock the heat was intense and easing myself into the water a real blessing.

Afterwards as we all sat chatting by the side of the pool, we turned idly to see Raymond coming up the lane on a tractor with one of the local boys riding at his side. He was carrying a large round bale of straw on the fork at the back. They were talking animatedly and had not noticed what we as they drew level could clearly see; the thin plume of smoke rising from the bale of straw.

We waved and shouted. Raymond beamed and waved back. We gesticulated. He laughed and shook his head. No, he didn't have time for a swim. We yelled again and pointed at his load. Grinning he shouted something incomprehensible about the destination of the bale which was now really beginning to burn. Frantically we jumped up and down as Hugh raced down the steps to the road. At last Raymond, realising that all this arm waving was not simple *bonhomie*, leapt down from the tractor, gawped, threw his arms into the air, sprang back up and dropped the by now crackling bale into the road. It rolled over against the bank which immediately caught fire. The wind began to whip the flames across the edge of the nearest field. It was all hands to every available shovel until *les pompiers* arrived to put out Raymond's burnt offering. 'And I thought what a jolly time *les Anglais* were having,' he said, laughing about it that evening.

A few days later, realising that the kilo of fresh peas we had just brought home from Villeneuve market might well be the last of the season, we made pigs of ourselves. In the middle of the night I began to regret it. I rolled about groaning while Mike made lemon tea and hot water bottles.

'Right,' he said. 'That's it. I'm going to order a telephone tomorrow.'

'Why?'

'You might have appendicitis!'

'It's just *trop de petits pois* I tell you!'

'Well – it might be appendicitis next time!'

'But what about the poles and the wires?'

We had been through this argument before. The best view from Bel-Air was to the south, down across what Raymond always called *le grand champ*, and the orchards. We could see for miles and miles and although there were, inevitably, in the far distance both telephone and electricity wires, there were none nearby to mar this special landscape.

'But what about the view?' I pleaded once more.

'And what if one of us has a heart attack?' asked Mike. There was no answer to that. I suddenly felt very vulnerable.

It was amazingly easy to get a telephone. We filled in the appropriate form and in a few days we were visited by the chief engineer. He measured the distance up the track.

'What a wonderful view you have up here – *c'est exceptionnel!*' he said.

'Yes,' I answered sadly. 'That's why we've not had a telephone before.'

He looked thoughtfully round and tapped his teeth with his pen.

'*Oui, ça serait vraiment dommage.*' He smiled suddenly. 'I think we might be able to preserve your view for you,' he said. 'If we were to bring the poles up to here,' he indicated the edge of the plum orchard, 'we could use the existing electricity post and cut across here, high up.'

I couldn't believe my luck.

'Is that possible?' I asked.

'*Tout est possible, chère Madame,*' he said, scribbling on a pad before whizzing away. The following week we received a letter to say that the telephone engineers would arrive in ten days' time and the installation would cost about twenty pounds. What service!

As my faith in the *guérisseuse* was waning fast and Corinne's parents had given me the name of a chiropractor in Agen, I decided that I would try him and christen my new telephone by making a rendezvous.

While we awaited the possibility of phoning friends, the village was getting ready for its annual fête to be held on the following Saturday night. The tickets were now on sale. Strictly speaking we are part of the adjoining commune but this is Raymond's village and our nearest and we usually all go together to any special event. This year it was to be a *mechoui*, a custom originally imported into France from North Africa, where a whole lamb is barbecued. It has become very popular in France, but for our fête, the village had chosen to roast a pig.

'Should we buy your tickets as well?' I asked Claudette on my way down to the shop. She shook her head enigmatically. They were not going it seemed ...

'*Mais pourquoi?*'

'*Parce que,*' she shrugged. And that was all I could get out of her. Something was up.

We had had the odd conversation about a certain dissatisfaction with the very close re-election, a few months previously, of their new Mayor. We knew that there had always been friction between him and some of the local farmers. Everyone's preoccupation with the wedding had clearly just postponed the problem and we now learned that not only was the village divided but that Raymond was the leader of the breakaway faction. What was it all about?

There was much shrugging and muttering but also a strong undercurrent of defiant excitement. Now we were told that plans were already afoot for an 'alternative' fête on the Sunday to which we were eagerly invited. As the last thing we wanted to do was to take sides it looked as though we had to go to both.

'Yes, it might be better for you to go to the official one as well,' agreed Claudette. 'It's not your quarrel, after all.'

The Mayor of our commune is a farmer and highly respected by everyone but in this adjoining commune Raymond's new Mayor is neither, and here begins I suspect, most of the trouble.

He is certainly an interesting, youngish man. Thin and pale with a mop of straw-coloured hair he speaks and sings in Occitan. He plays the fiddle. He does the occasional broadcast on local radio. He is keen on local history. But he is not a farmer and he is, so it is said, too keen on politics. There are even rumours – probably quite unfounded – about his having been trained in Cuba!

Local government in small communes is not usually party political. In fact as I write there are more than sixty candidates for the coming election of the Mayor of Villeneuve-sur-Lot, our nearest town of any size.

'Anyone can stand if they think they can do the job. *C'est la démocratie,*' said a friend of Raymond's proudly. '*Mais, c'est tellement chèr,*' he added less enthusiastically. '*C'est la commune qui doit payer.*'

But whatever skills the Mayor of Raymond's village has, the one he sadly lacks is the ability to unite the community behind him.

Alors! two *fêtes* in one weekend. Were we up to it? '*On verra,*' as they say round here.

On the Saturday evening we went down to the village just after eight o'clock. On the patch of ground next to the school, long tables and benches were ready and a dance-floor laid. As there was a threat of rain it was all crudely roofed over with plastic, but open at the sides. The air was sultry and filled with the smell of garlic and herbs and of the slowly roasting pork in the field behind, where children, racing about with wild shrieks, were chased away by the cooks. Music surged from loud speakers and we were greeted by everyone including the Mayor, who seemed very cheerful.

Intrigued to know just who was there, we were surprised to see that Raymond's nearest neighbour, also a farmer, was sitting at the first table. But then we remembered that his wife was a councillor. The wife of another close neighbour was the Mayor's secretary – we began to realise how complicated it was to have a feud in so small a village. We unpacked our plates and cutlery, which we had to bring, and stepped over the bench to sit down. M. René, the builder, and his wife shouted a greeting as they staggered in with a crate of individual cartons of rice salad with tuna, hard boiled eggs and tomatoes.

Ruth and Edward Thomas arrived with their grandson and a friend, both at school at Bryanston and both called Richard. The two blond, blue eyed young men had never been to such a gathering but were soon at ease, downing the unlimited sangria underneath the swaying, Heath Robinson strings of ordinary lightbulbs looped above the crowded tables. More and more people arrived and there was much kissing and squeezing closer together along the benches.

A great cheer went up as the meal started. To the usual ribaldry which seems to follow her around Mme Barrou, a local farmer's wife never at a loss for words, pushed her way through the tightly packed crowd with trays of melon. Hunks of bread landed on the tables. René came round yet again with huge jugs of sangria.

'You have to drink it all in one go,' he shouted.

'*Et glou et glou et glou*,' yelled everyone else in agreement, as the two young Richards – already nick-named *Les Coeurs de Lion*, – grew rosier by the minute. Fortunately there was plenty to eat. The delicious rice salad – 'We've been making it all afternoon,' beamed Mme René – was followed by melon and unlimited slices of pizza. Then the great moment arrived.

Two young men, their normally dark faces even darker with sweat and smoke, strode in, one behind the other. They lifted high the iron pole which skewered the glistening and aromatic roasted pig. They were followed by Joël, *le boucher*, who to riotous cheers brandished his great knife before ceremoniously leading off the pig to be cut up. His dark-eyed wife smiled sexily at him. I saw that she had had her long hair fashionably trimmed but was just as luscious as ever and there was a small dark replica on her lap.

Litres of local wine in plastic bottles were plonked onto the tables wherever there was a space as the portions of meat were served. There was a great choosing of favoured cuts, of slices less or more cooked, with or without fat, according to taste, before the bending to the serious task in hand. As it became quieter the music could now be heard and there were sighs of pleasure and much licking of fingers before a green salad finally appeared.

Large slabs of Cantal were passed down the table. I find it sad that this cheese which looks so like cheddar, tastes, to me at least, of nothing. I have to admit that when I want a strong hard cheese in France I turn to Holland and often buy *du vieux Gouda* in the market. It is difficult to cut but the taste is wonderful.

A rumble of thunder heralded one of those sudden downpours which are often part of the summer here. People rushed to cover the disco equipment while others fetched plastic fertiliser sacks with *AGRILOT* stamped on them and with the rain running off their brown faces pinned them up in a crazy, flapping row at the windward end. The rain didn't last long and as most of the revellers were glad that their maize, plums, vines and gardens were getting a free *arrosage* it did nothing to dampen their spirits.

While some of the young men appeared to be still on their third or fourth helping of the pig we were served ice-cream, and coffee with *eau-de-vie*. As the rain finally stopped, the covers came off the speakers and turntable and the dancing began, a buxom young woman carried in a huge crate of green-gages – just in case anyone was still hungry.

The pounding of many feet soon dried the steaming dance-floor. The Mayor made a short speech and asked us to greet the only part of the pig we had not cut up.

Joël, *le boucher*, brought in a brown, grinning pig's head. He cradled it lovingly in his hands and as he passed between the tables people kissed its roasted snout. For me, as so often happens, the time warp rippled and the

31

amplified beat of the music seemed to change to the squeak of more ancient instruments. The faces were the same, faces with strong features and expressions that would look out of place in a city. Round, dark, no Normans these, but people of the *'Langue d'Oc'*, people of the south who were so cruelly treated in the days when medieval France was still striving to become one kingdom.

We left them dancing and, as we lay in bed, listening for the odd mosquito, we heard the distant soft thud of revelry across our usually silent fields.

And of course the next day we had to do it all over again!

As it was Sunday, the opposition intended to make a whole day of it and we were invited for midday. As we arrived *chez Raymond* we saw about a dozen cars already parked. A large white refrigerated van was humming in the courtyard. Grandpa was leaning on his stick watching the unloading of yet another *grand repas*.

'What's going on?' we asked him.

'Don't ask me! *Moi, je ne sais rien,*' he shrugged. He turned away. *'Je ne suis que la cinquième roue de la voiture.* I'm only the spare wheel,' he roared. And that was that. He clearly did not approve.

But everyone else seemed to be having a splendid time. They were the rebels, this was the first rebellion, and it was fun. Some of the people we knew, but others were strangers. We were introduced to farmers who lived on the other side of the commune, and to two former Mayors. Gradually we began to piece together the reasons for their anger.

Apparently the new Mayor's unpopularity with certain farmers had reached such a degree that a group of new candidates had presented themselves, including two or three women, for the elections both for Mayor and for the local councillors which had taken place a few months previously. Long ago in the days when his father-in-law had been fit enough to share the work of the farm,

Raymond had been Deputy Mayor and they had also persuaded him to stand with them for election.

'I told them I am much too busy' he said. '*Mais, qu'est ce que vous voulez?* You are the only one, they told me and so I let my name go forward.'

What on earth he would have done had he been elected I can't imagine, but the problem was not that they had been defeated but, that when the present Mayor and council had put up their own list of candidates they had printed above their column of names the fatal words *VOTEZ POUR DES GENS HONNÊTES.*

'*Et alors* – *figurez-vous*,' cried Raymond passionately.

'What does that imply about us?'

As the splinter group and their followers cheered and applauded and thumped the tables we could see that this show would run and run.

The meal was almost a replica of the night before, melon, rice salad with fish but this time there was lamb not pork. We were amused to see the cheery face of Joël the butcher once again, who was, apart from ourselves, the only one to attend both functions. Of course he was the only butcher but he was also the son-in-law of a former Mayor. As I said, it was complicated. Much later we relaxed in the shade while they organised *un grand concours de pétanque.*

As soon as it began Grandpa came into his own. When *les boules* appear, rheumatism, age and creaking bones vanish as if by magic. He had been given, for some *anniversaire* or other, a smart new case in which to carry his own set of shiny, metal *boules*. Wearing his large straw hat, he hurried out. His back straightened and his chin at a determined angle, he took his place. He didn't win but he got into the finals and many were the sparks that he drew from his daring drop shots. It was a very good day, but after a weekend of roast pig and lamb, salads and cheeses, sangria and unlimited wine, I doubt if we could have faced another *fête* the following day.

5

That night a wind got up and as we lay in bed, once again we debated what to do about the little eddies of dust that were falling on us from the attic. When we first bought Bel-Air the ceiling of the small room which we enlarged into our bedroom was panelled with pine. We removed this false ceiling, not only because it was sagging and home to many legions of woodworm but also because we found it hid the beautiful oak beams and the original hand cut boards above.

It was these same hand-tongued and grooved oak boards which were now causing the trouble. It was probable that they had been there for at least two hundred years, perhaps longer. Some, less strong than others, had gradually succumbed to the woodworm, and the fact that the house had been uninhabited and neglected for eleven years before we found it can't have helped. Each year, as rain came through the roof, the boards had warped a little more, enlarging the gaps between them. Sadly it looked as though the time had come to replace them.

'Try M. Lecours,' advised Raymond, 'but you'd better get a move on if you want it done this year.'

'Why?'

He laughed. 'Because once the pigeon shooting starts ... work stops. *C'est sa passion!*'

M. Lecours was a short dark man with shifty eyes and a huge belly. He spoke very quickly out of the side of his mouth which he opened as little as possible. In spite of his girth he was as agile as a monkey and in spite of his eyes as honest as anyone would wish. He clambered all over the attic. Yes, the boards were very old. You could patch them but they would keep on moving. It would be better to replace the oak with chestnut, not pine, which the worms apparently preferred. Mind you, it was going to be difficult to level the ancient beams but he and his son would do their best. He took measurements and promised to come with a *devis*, an estimate, in a few days.

The next day we drove to Toulouse airport to collect my cousin David and Dorothy his mother. We usually ask our visitors to find their own way at least to Agen, if not to Villeneuve, but Dorothy had recently celebrated her eightieth birthday. As she had never been to this part of France we wanted her first impressions to be good ones. So on the way back we left the motorway at Montauban. It is one of the absolute joys of motoring in France that while most of the traffic thunders down the main roads there are small and enchanting, but good roads, unrolling an almost traffic-free network all over the country. For the sake of an extra ten or fifteen kilometres on a journey, often less, you can motor peacefully without passing another car in an hour. The only possible disadvantage is that anyone coming in the opposite direction doesn't expect to see you either.

Once through the industrial side of Montauban the road begins to climb. We crossed the Aveyron and the sunlight splintered as we entered the magnificent alley of plane trees at Loubejac. The trunks were bare, the lower branches lopped, but the feathery tops laced together across the road. Dorothy looked out eagerly as one fertile valley succeeded another with orchards of peaches, apples and hazelnuts, and patchwork fields of grain and maize and millet. The fragrant smell of burning sawdust from a timber merchant filled our nostrils as we came down from the ridge into yet another valley only to climb up again to the small town of Molières. We stopped to admire the view from high up above the lake, then drove on past Castlenau-Montratier with its huge, domed church, through Montcuq, its castle silhouetted against the burning blue sky, on past vine-yards and fields of ripening sunflowers and, hardly touching a main road, we at last climbed the track to Bel-Air.

Dorothy got stiffly out of the car and looked around.

'It's all so beautiful,' she said. 'It's a feast.'

I could not disagree.

A few days later we were wakened by the sound of an unfamiliar machine. At the bottom of the track were two telephone engineers with a heap of poles and a mechanical auger. Like a giant's screwdriver, with a bit more than two metres long, it bored into our hillside, withdrew, and swung limply aside while each pole was hoisted and dropped into place. Using no spirit level they worked at speed. Although the third pole had a certain charm it was anything but straight, but, as promised they stopped the line at the edge of the orchard and, refusing an aperitif, they disappeared.

The following day two more men arrived with a roll of cable. The chief, a handsome, moustached rugby player, told of visits to Dewsbury and Bradford and tried out his charmingly idiosyncratic English, shinning up and down the poles with obvious pleasure while threading through what looked like a great string of liquorice. By mid-morning it was finished. His gold chain gleaming on his brown chest, he swung himself up into his van. 'Good afternoon!' he shouted. 'They'll bring your telephone tomorrow. All is connected.' It was – but not for long.

That very night there was a violent storm. The electricity failed. The wind raged outside. In the candlelight, David and I sang as many hymns as we could remember; he, being a priest, knowing many more than I. Dorothy sat placidly at the window watching the rain. Suddenly there was a loud crack. Lightning not only struck one of our new poles, splitting it in two, but also burned right through the cable. The next day, a fierce sun steamed the sodden fields. The engineer arrived, telephone in hand, to finally connect us, and his face fell. However, to our surprise it was all mended by the end of the week, Bel-Air was 'on the phone' and I was able to make a rendezvous with the chiropractor.

The first person to   st on my bringing an X-ray to the initial consultation, he gave me a certain confidence. His surgery made that of my osteopath in London look like something out of Dickens and I began to feel he really might help me. As August passed I made three or four visits and at last was able to walk from one end of the market to the café in the middle by sitting down every few yards on the nearest garden wall.

'I'm sure the swimming helps,' I said to Mike.

'Wouldn't it be wonderful if we had our own pool?'

We talked about it with Hugh who is always an enthusiast.

'Spoil yourselves,' he urged, working out, I'm not exactly sure how, that it would cost us about sixty pence a day for the rest of our lives.

I had often dreamed of having a pool for the very hot summers but it was not just the cost which made us hesitate. We had tried so hard to *garder le style* of this very old and simple house. Bel-Air and a swimming pool seemed totally incompatible and yet, and yet ... that in itself had become a sort of challenge.

We walked across our rough meadow to the farthest edge and looked down across *le grand champ* to where the hills beyond the Lot valley begin.

'Look at the view you'll have from the pool,' said Hugh. 'It's the best view from Bel-Air and yet you never sit here.'

It was true. We had made terraces near the house to the south and to the west but the meadow was only used for a badminton court when anyone could be bothered to paint the lines. I had made no attempt to plant anything there, having always had an idea at the very back of my mind that if one day we did manage a pool, then I could finally plan a garden around it.

We began to give it serious thought, and to look more closely at every pool we saw. I started drawing on scraps of paper and marking with a cane exactly how far the shadow from the house came across the meadow as the evening sun went down.

But the pool was for the future. The immediate problem was the bedroom ceiling. Would M. Lecour *et fils* be able to fit it in before the open season for pigeons?

'*Ça dépend,*' said Raymond grinning.

'On what?'

'On whether they need the money at the moment.'

Fortunately it seemed that they did, as father and son appeared next morning, took final measurements, and said they would start in two days time.

Now all we had to do was move everything out of our bedroom and the adjoining corridor as the ancient boards covered both areas. Being slightly worried about an activity hardly recommended for sciatica, I was very relieved when Raymond arrived on the tractor to help us.

M. Lecour and his son worked very fast, smoked furiously and spoke hardly at all. We piled the old oak boards outside on the west terrace; just what we would need for next spring's fires. It was odd to be able to look straight up through the beams to the chinks of sunlight coming through the roof tiles. M. Lecour patted the great old beams fondly as he scrambled about from one to the other. We were sad to lose our original boards but, once in place, the new chestnut flooring looked pretty and smelled good.

When we eventually moved back into our bedroom it was a relief to know that our nights of diving under the covers to avoid the falling dust whenever the wind got up, were finally over.

It was finished just in time for we were expecting two more sets of guests. Our oldest friends, Tony White, and Nan his wife were driving down in stages from Northumberland and *les Fostaires*, as Raymond calls them, were coming from different directions, Judith from the Vercors where she had been learning about the growing and harvesting of plants for essential oils and Barry from London, although he had just finished filming in Provence.

Les Fostaires arrived safe and sound but sadly one of our first calls on our new telephone was to tell us that Tony had suffered a brain haemorrhage as he and Nan drove through Brittany. He had been rushed to hospital in Rennes. We were all stunned by the news. We thought about him most of the day and phoned each evening. His daughter and son-in-law flew out to support Nan and at least it seemed that he was holding his own. It was late September and, ironically, the weather was perfect.

Unable to help in any practical way we decided to continue with a proposed trip to Conques, about which we had heard a great deal.

'*On dit que c'est magnifique*,' said Raymond.

'But you've never been?'

'*Oh, un de ces beaux jours*,' he smiled and went off to finish yet another task.

The next day we set off with *les Fostaires*, following the Lot valley eastward. We made a small detour, being unwilling to miss that special moment when the great

Château of Bonaguil first towers into view against the thickly wooded hillside. The restaurants and, now, the horse drawn holiday caravans which cluster at its feet do little to diminish its grandeur.

Leaving the valley of the Lot we followed another smaller road which twists beside the river Célé, its banks lined with outcrops of rock which sparkle in the sunlight. This is schist: cut into curved tiles it makes the rooves of the houses glisten like the tails of mermaids.

We stayed the night at Figeac and late that evening phoned the hostel where Nan was staying. Being told she was still waiting at the hospital I feared the worst and rang.

'*Ne quittez pas,*' repeated a soothing voice as they searched for the extension number and in between there were bursts of soaring, solemn music as if to prepare one for bad news. Finally we were put through and after speaking to Nan we were thrilled to hear a very tired but lucid Tony talking about some poems he had taped and had been bringing for us.

'You will get them darling,' he said. We learned that there were plans to fly him back to England as soon as possible and that a difficult and dangerous operation was to follow. His chances were not good.

It seemed an appropriate time to be taking our road, insignificant on today's map but in the Middle Ages very important – the pilgrims way to Conques and the shrine of Saint Faith.

We reached it next day. The silver roofs sparkled beneath yet another cloudless sky and we walked around enchanted.

The village nestles, protected on all sides by high wooded plateaux. Originally a monastery it was given its present name of Conques – meaning a cavity – by Louis, King of Aquitaine and son of Charlemagne. Founded by an early Christian hermit, the remote monastery became famous in the ninth century when the relics of Saint Faith – *Sainte Foy*, a twelve-year-old girl, murdered for her faith some six hundred years earlier – were transferred from Agen. This assured the prestige of Conques for the next two centuries. Many miracles were reported and pilgrims staged at Conques on the way to Compostella.

We were lucky that day for the village was magically quiet and we learned that the following week it would be crowded for the annual procession.

Conques possesses the largest treasure of medieval gold in all France yet we looked at it almost alone. It is breathtaking, but for me, the history of the people of Conques throughout the centuries is just as fascinating.

In 866, to house the precious bones of the little saint, the inhabitants made a hollow wooden statue of yew, almost a metre high, and covered it with gold. For the head of the statue they used something they already had to hand, something much older.

It was discovered in 1955 that this head of embossed gold dates from the fourth century and originally wore a laurel wreath. Whose head it actually represented remains a mystery. The saint's skull was put inside and the wreath replaced with a crown. It was then crudely fitted onto the statue's wooden neck, tilting backwards. It is slightly too big for the body and it gives the statue, or 'majesty' as it is properly called (for she sits upon a splendid throne) a curious power.

The cult of Sainte Foy de Conques spread throughout Christendom into Italy and Spain, even to Horsham in England, and by the middle of the fourteenth century there was a village of some 3000 inhabitants, a flourishing market, and workshops in both gold and enamel. Pilgrims brought precious stones, rock crystals and sapphires and cameos to adorn the strange little figure with the enamel eyes of deepest blue. But she was only a part of a great golden treasure housed at Conques.

Although there was a gradual decline in the following

centuries with the ravages of the Black Death and the miseries of the Hundred Years War, Conques fared better than other shrines by being so hidden away.

During the wars of religion in 1568 the Calvinists destroyed part of the village. Fearing for their relics the inhabitants put most of the saint's bones inside two chests and built them into a wall between two columns in the church. There they remained.

By the end of the eighteenth century Conques was a very sad and different place. Famine and plague had taken its toll and the priest wrote of the remaining 630 inhabitants; 'we have 100 beggars in the parish ... to suffer from hunger, to live on chestnuts ... such is our situation.' During the revolution, with the abolition of all religious orders, its citizens lost the last help they had relied on. This poverty makes all the more remarkable their great act of faith.

After the revolution in 1794 the National Convention ordered the confiscation of all precious metal objects to be melted down and many of France's greatest ecclesiastical treasures were destroyed. But once more the inhabitants of Conques took their treasures and hid them; this time in chimneys, chestnut stores, attics and stables, and simply waited for the political storms to pass.

It was the young Prosper Merimée, newly appointed as the first Inspector General of historical monuments, but more famous today as the author of Carmen, who was sent on a journey which eventually led him to Conques.

One can only imagine his astonishment after riding into that remote, poverty stricken village when the people took him on a tour of their hiding places to show him all the priceless things they had so carefully guarded. He it was who in 1838 alerted the State and praised the brave *citoyens* of Conques for their courage and their honesty.

The only thing that perplexed the experts of the time was the lack of bones inside the statue. Some village elders claimed that the bones were said to have been buried in the church. The strange wall between two pillars behind the altar was demolished and on 21 April 1875, a wooden chest was discovered containing the missing bones all intact and a coin dated 1590. After almost two hundred years the bones of the little martyr were once again reunited.

I don't know whether it was anything to do with Sainte Foy but by the end of that September my sciatica had finally gone and Tony had had his operation and was well on the way to a complete, and pretty miraculous, recovery.

6

We returned from Conques in time for the second day of *les vendanges* the picking of the grapes. When we first bought Bel-Air Raymond made his own red and white wine. At that time we would drive back to England with a large wicker covered glass *bidon* containing what he called *mon petit vin* and bottle it as soon as we arrived. Now, all his grapes for *le vin rouge* go to the *Co-opérative* and it is they who specify the days for the receiving of the different grapes, this day for the Merlot, another for the Sauvignon.

Les Fostaires joined us for this, the last day of their holiday and we picked the grapes in the vineyard on the other side of the hill, which had once belonged to Bel-Air. The view is glorious and from the top of the long, south-facing slope the Château of Biron can be seen on the horizon. We were among about twenty pickers: neighbours, friends and family and, as always, Mme Barrou was there, wielding the heavy baskets as easily as the men and talking non-stop. Mike had woken that morning with a stiff neck, or *torticolis*, as we learned it was called. As usual Mme Barrou had a remedy.

'*Il faut une tisane de cassis*,' she yelled down the row of vines. '*Et de la graisse de marmotte.*'

A tisane of blackcurrant sounded harmless enough but marmot grease? The taste was unimaginable. '*Graisse de marmotte?*' I enquired.

'*Oui. J'en ai toujours chez moi. Pour le torticolis – c'est impeccable!*' She did a quick mime of massaging her neck.

'I see. But ... where do you get it?' I asked. Mme Barrou looks capable of both trapping and rendering down a marmot or two but I wasn't sure that I was – even if I could find any.

'*A la pharmacie*,' she said as though it was a silly question and she moved on with her basket. 'Mind you,' she called over her shoulder. 'You have to keep it on for eight days and it smells a bit.'

Everyone laughed and I began to wonder if marmot grease was like striped paint or sky hooks.

A few days later I was at market and, to get back to the car, I had to pass the pharmacy. The stiff neck was gone but I was curious. Chemist's shops in France are rather like operating theatres with shelves, the assistants usually formal in their immaculately white coats. The one who greeted me looked more than capable of advanced neuro surgery.

'*Bonjour Madame, vous désirez?*'

I bought some toothpaste then swallowed. '*Et ... de la graisse de marmotte s'il vous plâit. C'est pour ma voisine*,' I lied. Implying, I hoped, that it was not I who was mad. The blue eyes behind the rimless glasses did not even flicker.

'*En pot ou en emplâitre?*' she enquired briskly, turning towards the row of small white drawers behind her.

'*Er ... en emplâitre?*' I said not having the faintest idea what it was.

She pulled from a drawer a plastic envelope about a foot

wide with a plaster inside and a picture of a furry animal on the front. I paid and left the shop. I am still waiting for someone to get a stiff neck in order to try it out.

Our last guests had gone. We too would soon begin packing up the house but there was one more *vendange* to be completed. Raymond and Claudette still make their own sweet white dessert wine. It is rather like a Monbazillac, and they serve it with a biscuit on those evenings when we go down to watch something special on television, or just to sit and chat. They use an ancient *pressoir* which Grandpa tells me he bought in 1921 to trundle round the neighbouring farms to make a little extra money. The old barrel that they had used in previous years having finally fallen to pieces, Raymond had bought a 'new' second-hand barrel the week before. It had been filled with water and left to swell to forestall any possible leaks.

That morning the grapes we picked were *semillon*, *sauvignon blanc*, and a few *chasselas* – really a grape for eating – to make up the bulk. Some of the *semillon* looked mouldy to me but Raymond raised his eyebrows at my ignorance. He assured me that this was the highly prized noble rot – *la pourriture noble* – which makes the grapes dry and concentrates the sugar. He explained that the most famous Sauternes, Château d'Yquem, is made from grapes affected in this way. In this case, however, the pickers must only take each day those grapes which have begun to rot and leave the others. Costs are correspondingly very high and most small *producteurs* pick, as we did, on one day and hope for as much noble rot as possible.

It was not a large crop and we went back to the farm with the trailer only about three quarters full. The ancient *pressoir* stood in the courtyard. Like a very large straight-sided barrel, the narrower than usual wooden staves were encircled with three iron hoops with metal struts angled between them. There was a large screw in the centre which would press down the heavy wooden block. The whole thing was mounted on a crude, rusty iron chassis and propped up on a pile of bricks. A lopsided ancient half-barrel stood beneath the spout to catch the juice. It was clear that many litres had passed through this system.

Grandpa came slowly across the courtyard and gazed at it with a far away expression but he said nothing until Mike, looking inside, said 'There's a lot of old wood in it.' Then he laughed. He explained that these were in fact carefully cut pieces to fit under the pressing weight when there were not enough grapes. Grandma had come silently to join him. 'Ah yes,' she said 'sometimes ... when the harvest was bad.'

Before he began the pressing Raymond remembered that he had not yet emptied the new barrel. 'I'd better do that first,' he muttered, tipping it up. It was then that he discovered that there was no bung at either end on which to fit a tap for the eventual bottling. *'Je n'ai pas remarqué ça – merde, merde, merde!'* he cursed, rolling the barrel back and forth before running off to return with a very bent brace and an old bit. With Mike's help a hole was carefully drilled and corked before everything was hosed down, the *pressoir*, the barrel and a large copper pan.

'That pan's old enough for a museum,' he shouted. To me it all looked old enough for a museum.

With a grin Raymond slipped off his espadrilles and climbed up into the trailer.

'What about hosing your feet?' I called.

'Non,' he laughed. *'Ca donne du goût!'* That adds to the taste!

The grapes roughly trampled down, he climbed out and backed the tractor up over a block of wood, the better to tip the trailer of grapes into the *pressoir*. As a thin stream of juice began to run from the bottom we turned the screw, first with a short handle, then a longer one to get greater leverage, until the two nodding donkey ratchets dropped into a slot with a loud clack. Everyone had a try and it was hard work. We tasted the juice which frothed into the half barrel. It was sweet. 'We shan't need to add any sugar this year' said Raymond. The juice was put into the barrel in the cave where it would be allowed to ferment for about six weeks. When the sugar level reached 3-4% the fermentation process would be stopped by the addition of a little liquid sulphur. After two years in the barrel the wine would be bottled in clear glass bottles. Occasionally they find a bottle at the back of the cave which has been forgotten. Often it must be tipped down the sink, leaving a brown sticky residue, but sometimes it is a clear, deep golden colour and tastes more like fortified wine than merely the product of simple grapes from our hillside.

Before leaving that summer we made a decision about the pool. There didn't seem a great deal of point in leaving our savings for old age, which seemed all too close. The fact that a pool would cost about the same as an average family car but, unlike the car, would increase in value, finally clinched it. We both love to swim, even in London, Mike every day in our local leisure centre and I twice a week. Our own pool in France to use throughout the summer was to become, at last, not just a distant fantasy but a reality.

M. Bourrière who runs *Piscine* 47 at Villeneuve sur Lot, (47 being the number of the *départment* of Lot-et-Garonne) had come up to examine our sloping meadow. A rotund, curly haired figure in cowboy boots he strode about through the rough grass and commented on our *point de vue* as he took a few measurements and discussed the position of the pool and where he would put the pump.

'Over here in this far corner I think,' he said marching off again, trailing us behind him. 'I'll set it into the ground. All you will see is the green plastic cover and you can soon grow something to hide it.' He took a few more notes then shook hands. '*Pas de problème*,' he smiled, climbing into his van which sagged heavily to one side. He promised to send us all the details, and if we finally agreed, to be ready to begin when we arrived in the following spring and to have it all finished by July.

He seemed extremely casual about what was to us a major undertaking but Raymond assured us that all would be well for M. Bourrière's family was known locally; indeed long ago his father had once been the mayor.

'That was in the days when being mayor meant something,' he added darkly. We'd finally done it! Raymond shared our excitement. He swam occasionally in our friends' pools but this would be often, as it were, on his way from work.

'I shall be able to practise every day,' he cried. 'I shall become a champion swimmer.'

Claudette laughed. 'When will you find the time?' she said. 'And anyway, it takes you twenty minutes to get in.'

It was true. Even on the hottest day Raymond lowered himself into a pool inch by inch gasping all the while. In vain we all pleaded with him to at least try another system, but once in, his delight with his new experience was boundless.

At the end of October we received *le devis* from France and were plunged into the technical world of the construction and furnishing of a swimming pool. There was a great deal of searching the dictionary.

M. Bourrière sent us samples of *le liner* in various shades of blue, and we chose the palest, having noted on our researches of every pool we could get a look at that previous summer, that it gave the most reflection of the sunlight and, as a consequence, the 'Hockney' effect we wanted.

The pool was to be ten metres by five and we drew endless diagrams to decide exactly how far down the field to put it and how wide the surround should be. I was anxious that it would, eventually, blend in with the garden but the south facing edge would have to be at least three metres wide to accommodate chairs and tables, and as the sun went round, the west facing edge also would have to be wider than the remaining two.

M. Bourrière's estimate was in four parts; the earthworks, the construction of the pool, the pool finishing and the finishing of the surround. On the first page there was a price for the actual digging of the hole and another for the landscaping of the excavated earth but there was an ominous blank space for figures by an item described as *brise roche en supplément s'il y a lieu*. After consulting the dictionary yet again we fervently hoped that there wouldn't be too many rocks to be smashed up, making it necessary to pay a supplement! As for the surround we decided to have just the basic cement until we could decide exactly on the finished surface. We didn't want to make 70 square metres of mistakes. We sent off our ten per cent deposit and were now committed.

I took the photographs I had taken of Bel-Air to my publisher only to learn that as a cost-cutting exercise they would not, after all be included in the book. Within weeks Allison and Busby had been taken over yet again, this time by Virgin, most of the staff had been sacked and my manuscript was put on hold. 'Trust me,' said my editor Peter Day. 'It will be published.' And, thanks to him it was – but not for another eighteen months, appearing two weeks after Peter Mayle's second book about Provence: not the most fortuitous timing. But any disappointments about the book were completely forgotten in the plans for the pool. Letters went back and forth and we arranged to be at Bel-Air at the beginning of April when the work would start ...

When we arrived that spring, it was bitterly cold. I sewed loops on a blanket and we hung it inside the front door to keep out the north wind which tore round the house. We gave thanks for the new bedroom ceiling and the ever dimi nishing pile of old oak boards on the west terrace whic h kept the fire going continuously. Down on the farm every one was wrapped in layer upon layer and, although the fields were bright with daffodils, Raymond was gloomy about the chances of the wheat germinating; there had been no rain. Huddled round the open fire, it seemed extremely odd to be thinking about swimming pools, but after a few days the icy wind suddenly dropped and soon we were peeling off the layers.

Each day we started gardening in a track suit, sweater, socks and boots; by midday it was espadrilles, shorts and a sun top. Later, as the light began to fade, we would gradually reclaim the discarded clothes and stoke up the fire. All my aches and pains of the previous summer had gone and being able to walk and dig, bend, stretch, push, lift and stride about the garden was a joy. It was also fun to have a telephone: even Claudette found it useful. She would often ring to ask me to shout to Raymond across the field that someone had arrived to see him.

We cooked Sunday lunch for the family; minestrone, followed by smoked trout brought from our favourite fishmonger in the Wandsworth Road in London, and steak and kidney pie with a great variety of vegetables. As usual Claudette tucked into everything and Raymond tasted and considered and asked questions before making up his mind. Grandpa loved the trout. He is very fond of all fish.

At last came the call that we were waiting for. *La pelle*, the digger, would arrive the next day. We now knew what to expect unlike all those years ago when we had thought that *la pelle* meant a shovel attached to a man, and had been absolutely amazed to see the great mechanical digger struggling up our track to dig out the pathway round the house.

M. Bourrière arrived first with an assistant and a great deal of measuring and sighting went on, as the meadow sloped southwards. Wooden pegs were hammered in at each corner with the levels marked in red. The long side of the pool would face south and as he was explaining how the earth would be banked up along the lower edge, the approaching noise of the digger could be heard. We all went to meet it and to be introduced to M. Gibelou, a sweet-faced young man who turned out, as so often happens, to be a distant cousin, this time of Claudette. I took a last look at the meadow, rough, wild and patched with yellow coltsfoot – as Anaïs would have known it. It would never be the same again.

Any momentary sadness was soon forgotten in the excitement of the digging. A great rectangle of grass was hurled aside and a metre of good rich topsoil was revealed, most of it, I imagine, washed down from the top of the hillside over long years. Carefully conserved in a great pile at the bottom of the meadow, it soon dwarfed our low, sloping-rooved house. Underneath the soil was chalk and more chalk, some of it in huge blocks. We watched anxiously for signs of anything more solid but although the digger whined and grumbled it dealt swiftly with larger and larger blocks. M. Gibelou, clearly an expert, made a rough ramp with the chalky rocks on which to bump down into the excavated area.

Gradually the hole grew deeper and his last manoeuvre with the great machine was to make it clamber up out of the pool and dig out the ramp itself. The chalky undersoil was piled by the fence at the top edge of the field and, after an aperitif all round – except for M. Bourrière who, in spite of every appearance of enjoying all earthly pleasures, turned out not to drink alcohol – they all went home, leaving us to contemplate the large hole in our meadow. Raymond, who within ten minutes came up to inspect it, nodded approvingly at the separated pile of topsoil.

'You'll be able to get some good plants going in that later on,' he said.

Before coming in for a pastis he went down the track to the lower field to look at the wheat. *'Il faut de la pluie,'* he sighed shaking his head. That night, as if to order, brilliant sheet lightning flashed across the sky for hours and at last towards dawn the rain came, gently at first and then a steady downpour which continued all next day. There was no work done outside and as I dusted and polished all the furniture with beeswax I once again gave thanks for *France Musique*, the French equivalent of Radio Three. The programmes are much longer and for two hours I listened with great pleasure to several Oratorio by Handel with, among others, Robert Tear in glorious voice.

As we cooked supper that night, the Calor gas cylinder needed changing, and we discussed dispensing with gas altogether. The gas water heater which M. Albert the plumber had unaesthetically installed twelve years before to one side of a hand cut stone arch – and which we had ever since planned to move – needed constant attention because of the chalky water. I would also, I realised, be quite glad to see the back of my cooker, although I had learned to cope with the idiosyncrasies of French cookers which heat up the floor of the oven almost as hot as the top shelf. I had never cooked with electricity and I was willing to try, but we would, I knew, have to upgrade our electricity supply to the house. Unlike in England where one simply assumes that no matter how many appliances one switches on there will be sufficient power, in rural France it is a very different matter.

When we first bought Bel-Air in 1976, although it was on mains electricity, there were two lights only in the house. One had hung above the table, but was now a bare piece of flex, where previous viewers of the then derelict house had stolen the old lamp; the other, a soot-blackened bulb was fixed to the wall of the chimney making it possible for Anaïs to do much of her cooking over the fire. We made our first trip to an office of *Electricité de France* and the assistant looked with some amazement at our bill. The lowest installation on his hand written chart was 3kW and was described as *TARIF SIMPLE*. It seemed Bel-Air had only a 1kW supply. He shrugged, smiled and said that it appeared that for us he must invent a special category. He suggested '*TARIF PRIMITIF*.'

As the more kW one had the higher became the standing charge, we settled at that time for the *TARIF SIMPLE* and it became a running joke to turn off all the lights before boiling the kettle or using the washing machine. In any case if you did blow the fuse it was a simple matter to reset *le disjoncteur*, the circuit breaker, by pushing up a switch in the cupboard. This would at once reconnect the supply. It was clearly a necessary device in a country where blowing fuses must surely be a common occurrence.

The next day, although warm, it was still raining and we called in to see M. Albert the plumber who showed us photographs of his latest grandchild.

'How many have you got now?' we asked.

'Six,' he said proudly. 'And what a pleasure they are.'

We discussed the proposed electric water heater. He was enthusiastic. 'I'm getting tired of servicing that old geyser you've got,' he grinned. We talked about the pool and about changing to an electric cooker.

'No problem,' he said. 'But if you want my advice you should go onto the special tariff. It's called EJP.'

He wasn't too sure what the letters stood for but it seemed that it was a system for cheaper electricity. Off we went to investigate this EJP which we found stood for *Effacement Jour de Pointe*. The French export a great deal of electricity. In order to ensure an adequate supply in peak times, they have invented this scheme to persuade the home consumer to switch off when they deem it necessary. By taking part in this system, electricity is considerably cheaper all year round except for the possibility that on any one of twenty-two days in the year, '*Les Jours de Pointe*' between November 1 and March 31, when the demand may exceed the supply, they have the right to change the tariff. A red light indicator on the meter will show that now the charge will be almost ten times as much per kW – a real inducement to switch off!

I am constantly entertained by the language used in sales literature in France. The leaflet we were given was no exception ...

'Et bien, c'est pratiquement le tarif de nuit toute l'année, de jour comme de nuit sauf ... sauf une toute petite période pendant laquelle le prix de l'électricité sera plus cher. Voilà! Vous savez tout! A vous de choisir!' ('You see, it's almost the cheap night rate all year round, and all day long except ... except a very tiny period when the price of electricity will be dearer. There it is. Now you know everything. It is for you to choose!')

As we were very unlikely to be at Bel-Air between November and the end of March it seemed the perfect choice for us but we were surprised to learn that Raymond and Claudette were also on EJP. Was it economical? Claudette maintained that it had been so far. The *jours de pointes* were not allowed to run consecutively and so far had been very rare during the winter and had only lasted for a few hours. 'I leave the freezer shut and don't do any washing or ironing,' she said. *'C'est pas trop dur.'*

The last days of the Calor gas bottles and the installation of an all electric kitchen became something else for us to plan, as well as the everlasting debate about what to do with our large outhouse, or *chai*. With the certainty of having umbrellas and all the poolside paraphernalia to store would we be able to hive off a part of it for another bedroom as we hoped? And if we could, which way round should we do it? We started drawing yet more plans, wandering about with rulers and standing in the middle of the space and staring.

The weather improved and in a few days the next stage of the pool began. M. Gibelou and his digger had left and there were two different workmen in the crater, smoothing the rough surface and taking out the odd loose boulder. They fixed a central drain and dug a channel for the strong hose which would make the underground connection to the pump. The next day, wearing heavy gloves, they manhandled sheets of steel mesh with which they lined the bottom and sides of the crater and that afternoon the cement lorry arrived. Now it was a race between the two of them and the steady flow which poured from the long hydraulic arm. They were extremely skilful and gradually a rough chalky, stony hole was transformed into the shape of a swimming pool with the smoothness of an iced cake.

M. Bourrière arrived with his partner, Claudine – a name easy to remember being so near to 'chlorine', the essential chemical of pool maintenance – and they pronounced themselves satisfied. We wished that we could see the whole of the process but M. Bourrière explained that they would not begin the next stage for many weeks. We discussed the landscaping of the rest of the meadow. Claudine smiled.

'It will look terrible to begin with,' she said. 'But after one season – you will see – it will be beautiful.'

I looked at all the great muddy tracks across the field, the piles of boulders and the towering heaps of earth and hoped she was right.

As the next day was my birthday we went off to buy champagne and to order a large tart at the boulangerie. Raymond and Claudette and the two old people came up about nine o'clock. They brought me a callistemon or bottle brush plant and I planted it the next day in the south-facing bed. They sang *'Bon anniversaire'* and Grandpa pronounced the champagne good.

'Le champagne, bravo!' he roared. *'Mais ... vous savez ... aujourd'hui il y a plus de buveurs que de connaisseurs!'* We toasted the new swimming pool and the pleasure we hoped to have from it in the coming years.

7

Plans for an early return to Bel-Air that summer were postponed by my having what, in the theatre, is known as 'a spit and a cough', in the very first episode of the successful TV comedy series 'The Brittas Empire'. It was high summer, real swimming pool weather, but instead of setting off down the long straight roads of northern France, I was commuting to Acton. I must admit that I wasn't exactly sorry not to have a larger part, and by the second week in July, we were packed and ready to go. Although we had somehow fitted half a pine kitchen, an electric cooker and a ten foot worktop into our estate car we were determined not to put the car on the train this time, but to take several days over the journey and enjoy some as yet unexplored parts of France. The first place I wanted to visit was the Château of Nohant, the home of George Sand.

When we had first bought Bel-Air in 1976 I had soon realised that I would have to do something about my extremely limited French. I started in a beginner's class at

Morley College in South London and, thanks to imaginative teaching, made progress. The class which I subsequently joined had by now transformed itself, first into a French history class, then, leaving the college altogether, into an Anglo-French group of friends. For the last ten years we have much enjoyed studying, in both languages, the history of England and of France. That winter we had concentrated on the first half of the nineteenth century through the literature of the time and I had been completely captivated by George Sand.

My vague memories of a pallid Merle Oberon gazing languidly at the young Chopin in an old Hollywood film were quickly effaced. George Sand's portrait showed a strong beauty with great heavy-lidded eyes and her writing revealed a brilliant, feisty, and incredibly hard-working woman. She spoke with a frankness and an immediacy which delighted me. The famous relationship with Chopin was but one episode in an extraordinary life.

She was born in Paris as Aurore Dupin in 1804. Her father had aristocratic connections being the illegitimate grandson of the Maréchal de Saxe; her mother however was a camp follower, and the daughter of an itinerant bird seller. At the age of four, the little Aurore was dragged across war-torn Spain by her pregnant and impulsive mother, who was unable to wait for the return of her handsome soldier husband, fighting for Napoleon.

With her parents she came back to live with her grandmother in the family home at the Château of Nohant, which I was planning to visit. Within a year of their return, both the new baby and Aurore's father were dead, and the two bereaved women began their battle for the upbringing of the child. The mother, poor and uneducated, and with an earlier illegitimate daughter to support, was no match for her formidable and wealthy mother-in-law. In spite of many broken promises to come to collect her daughter she left for Paris and virtually sold the little girl for an allowance of 1000 F a year to her cold and correct paternal grandmother. George Sand wrote of her grandmother later 'I had a terrible fear of becoming like her and when she made me sit at her side without moving it seemed as though she was commanding me to die.'

Aurore's education was entrusted to her father's old tutor, Deschartes, who had been chosen for him by Voltaire and was himself a formidable person. He made no differences for her sex and taught her Latin, history and mathematics. But as she grew older she would escape and run wild with the village children, and her love and understanding of the countryside was to inspire much of her writing. Her grandmother, worried that she would be unable to make a good marriage, sent her to be educated at the English Convent of the Augustins, which had been established in Paris since the time of Cromwell. Some two thirds of the boarders were English, French was not to be spoken at certain hours and the predominantly Irish nuns drank tea three times a day. At first it was simply yet another traumatic change in her life, but she soon made friends and, having her own room, began the habit of writing and dreaming rather than sleeping at night. All her life she needed very little sleep. She described her time at the convent as being 'the most perfect happiness I had ever tasted in my life'.

At seventeen she was brought back to Nohant. Her grandmother was becoming old and infirm and it was now the task of Deschartes to instruct Aurore on the management of the estate. Wearing her father's riding clothes she would accompany Deschartes when he went to administer medicine or practise minor surgery in the nearby villages. She devoured the vast library reading at night to her grandmother with whom, at last, she established some rapport before the old lady died.

At eighteen she married Baron Casimir Dudevant and had two children but her unconventional behaviour and conversation outraged local society. No one thought it odd when her husband took mistresses but when she demanded the same sexual freedom it caused a scandal. After eight years of an increasingly unhappy marriage she left for Paris taking her daughter with her. She began to dress like a man simply for economy and for the freedom it gave her. The fashion at the time for young men was a long squarish 'sentry-box' coat which reached to the ankles. Under this were worn trousers, a waistcoat and what she enjoyed most of all, boots.

'I can't convey how much my boots delighted me: I'd have gladly slept in them,' she wrote. 'With those steel tipped heels I was solid on the pavement at last. I dashed back and forth across Paris and felt I was going around the world. I was out and about in all weather, came home at all hours, was in the pits of all the theatres.' These were all adventures which wearing women's clothes would have made impossible.

She had promised her husband's parents that she would not use her married name if she intended to do anything as vulgar as be published. Once again it was more convenient to take on the guise of a man and so 'George Sand' was born – a woman who would have many lovers, befriend many artists, support many causes and still find time to write over thirty novels and countless articles. As for her lovers she maintained ... *'pour être romancier, il faut être romanesque, comme il faut être lièvre pour devenir çivet'* which **very** roughly translated means 'to make a novelist one needs romance as to make a casserole one needs a hare!'

After her busy life in Paris George Sand returned to Nohant and there she entertained by day such distinguished contemporaries as Flaubert, Balzac, Delacroix, Liszt and Turgenev while writing each night from midnight until four a.m. to support an increasing group of friends and family ...

*

Mike and I stayed the night at Les Andelys, a sort of backwater loop of the Seine, in an old fashioned hotel. It made up in romantic charm and with the most delicious *'oeuf en cocotte au Roquefort'* for its lack of modern plumbing, having at that time, many quaint bedrooms but only one lavatory; and the next day we drove on. Nohant is just north of La Châtre. You must walk the last distance for no cars are allowed into the hamlet. It was a hot still afternoon. A dreamy young man was playing Chopin on a grand piano in the coach house and a great catalpa in flower towered over the Château. It is unpretentious, an elegantly proportioned stone manor house, with its fourteenth century church and small cottages. The house is preserved much as it was in George Sand's lifetime. Her grand-daughter lived there until she died in 1961 at the age of ninety-five.

The rooms in which George Sand wrote, slept and entertained still enshrine the piano at which both Liszt and Chopin composed. Her collection of the works of Voltaire, her books on geography, philosophy and her filing cabinets of fossils were all fascinating. Alas, the young guide had learned his lines and was eager to say them as fast as possible. I would have liked to stay and wander at my will, especially in the theatre where, often with Chopin's help, George Sand would try out her plays, casting them from friends, family and anyone she could persuade to take part. There is also a puppet theatre with one-hundred-and-sixty marionettes which her son Maurice made, and for which she designed and sewed most of the costumes. One leaves Nohant with an overwhelming impression of a life of such creative energy and yet, especially toward the end, an acceptance of its limitations. Content at last to write when she felt like it she amused herself by playing with and teaching her granddaughter, strolling in her garden and, until the year before she died, by swimming in the river.

We drove slowly away from Nohant through the

peaceful countryside and spoiled ourselves by finding a hotel by the side of a lake and eating the 180F menu. We drooled over a *terrine de légumes avec mousse de foie*, followed by a wonderful *entrecôte*, a salad, and then the best chocolate ice-cream I've ever tasted. It was almost black and covered in chocolate sauce in which were strips of caramelised orange peel. As we gazed out at the lakeside terrace with its elegant recliners and umbrellas, its small tables, and the lights reflecting in the moonlit water, we wondered exactly what we would see when we arrived at Bel-Air the next day.

I wrote in my journal – field a disaster, pool a triumph!

Mike went straight to telephone M. Bourrière to congratulate him on the immaculate sparkling blue rectangle in our devastated meadow, before we stripped off and enjoyed this first swim in our own pool. Now I was pleased that we hadn't been here to watch every stage as the surprise was so much a part of the fun. We spread towels on the concrete surround and dried off, but it was too hot to lie there for long without shade of some kind. We had always used the ash tree whenever we needed shade – now we would have to think about umbrellas.

We gazed around at the bare dusty earth, the heaps of stones and the once muddy tracks, now baked into solid ruts. Would the grass ever grow again? What on earth would Anaïs have thought of this extravagance, when she wouldn't even have a tap installed? Even as she and her son Aloïs grew increasingly old and frail they still drew all their water from the well in the porch. And the meadow? I knew how she had loved her garden. I was always finding odd little plantings, roses and lilac down by Raymond's pond, which had once been a part of our property, and irises by the barn wall. I resolved to make the ugly brown devastation into a beautiful garden even if it took me the next ten years.

It grew hotter. It was a perfect summer for swimming pools. Claudine came to give us a lesson in the necessary pool cleaning, hoovering, back washing and treating with chemicals. 'It's easy,' she reassured. *'Il faut aller doucement, doucement,'* she instructed as Mike wrestled with the long-handled brush. The cows in the next field were very interested in all this activity. There were nine heifers and an older cow, who was in charge. They stood in a row gazing over the wire and from a distance looked as though they were lining up to swim.

M. Gibelou returned in a few days to smooth out the tracks and to discuss the rearranging of the piles of earth. I wanted to protect the pool from the north wind in some way.

'You need a low wall,' he said 'I know just the chap to do it for you. He's a bit ...' he spread his hands and shrugged, 'but he understands stones. He'll do you a really good job ... *un joli petit mur*. Then I can bank up the earth to the wall and you can begin to plant.'

That was what I wanted to hear.

He returned that evening with the new *maçon*, M. Duparcq. He extolled his friend's skill at building *les jolis murs* while M. Duparcq shuffled his feet and said nothing. It reminded me of Steinbeck's *Of Mice and Men*, for M. Duparcq was a giant of a man. He had the longest legs I'd ever seen and wore the shortest shorts. A small, grubby white cotton hat shaded his eyes which peered out from a face as shapeless as a potato. A rough moustache hid his mouth. M. Gibelou encouraged him.

'It's not difficult, is it. You could soon get it done, eh?'

M. Duparcq surveyed the scene.

'I would like the wall made with old stones and perhaps curved at this end,' I said hopefully. There were already enough straight lines with the pool.

He nodded slowly. *'Oui,'* he said at last, *'la semaine prochaine.'*

The weather grew even hotter. The last few days of that week we wondered how we had ever managed without a pool in which to plunge every half-hour. The maize in the *grand champ* seemed to be fainting in the heat in spite of being watered and there was almost no water in the pond for the cows. Normally they trek down the field several times a day led by 'mother' but now each evening Raymond had to fill a trough under the ash tree with water for them to drink.

On Monday we saw our first cloud. It was a bit like the scene in *Jean de Florette* for it floated slowly over but dropped no rain and it was ninety degrees Fahrenheit under our north-facing porch.

'*C'est la canicule!*' yelled Grandpa as he drove past in his battered van. We hardly needed telling that there was a heatwave! Shopping had to be done in the early morning and our nearest town Monflanquin was full of music. This year was to be the sixth year of *Musique en Guyenne*, ten July days of study, by musicians of all ages and from all regions, who stay locally and have daily master-classes in guitar, brass, strings and woodwind. There is also a choir of 120 singers and each year the programme becomes more ambitious with recitals in nearby châteaux by international soloists. The standard of the students is extremely high and the final concert in the church at Monflanquin is always thrilling. The soloists that year for the Brahms Requiem included an American soprano with a wonderfully sure technique and a glorious voice and the church was packed to the roof.

On Sunday we went down to the farm for lunch. We only discovered when we got there that it was the anniversary of two weddings. Philippe and Corinne, was it a year ago already? And Raymond and Claudette too. They had kept very quiet about that the previous year. Although it was scorching outside we started as usual with soup, a light *consommé*, which never fails to whet the appetite and then tasted the first melons.

'There won't be many this year if it doesn't rain soon,' said Claudette.

She cut more bread and Grandma carried in the next course, a plate of thinly cut smoked salmon, a rare treat here. Next came a dish of baked *courgettes farcies* and roast guinea fowl. There was much reminiscing about past weddings, in the middle of which Grandpa announced that he and Grandma were married in 1931. If he said, he was still alive next year, they would be celebrating their diamond wedding. None of us could compete with that!

The next morning we were still in bed when M. Duparcq arrived to begin the wall. It was seven a.m. We were paying him ninety francs an hour and it certainly looked as though he was going to put in a long day. He unloaded a cement mixer and a pile of breezeblocks. *'C'est pour l'autre côté,'* he said stolidly. 'You won't see them at all.' I hoped not!

He had to hose the baked ground the length of the proposed wall several times before his pickaxe could make any impression and a trench could be dug. He curved it elegantly at the end and I began to have more confidence. Over the weeks we would learn that he was a very skilled and conscientious craftsman and his taciturnity was simple shyness. By Wednesday he had almost finished facing the breezeblock wall and it was looking really good. When we had first bought Bel-Air I had had a try at building the odd small stone wall to edge a flower bed. Now I watched a professional. He would sort out the stones from the surrounding heaps, weigh them in his huge hands and place them in exactly the right way. He inserted the odd piece of red tile here and there *'pour faire plus joli'* he said, and brought flat stones for the top of the wall. He told us that what we needed to finish the end nearest the house were several large blocks of stone which had already been cut. *'Les pierres d'angle, bien taillées,'* he explained, adding that there were several such stones lying in a heap by the ruin down past the pond. As these belonged to my neighbour

M. Ablard I asked Raymond for advice.

'I'm sure he'll sell you a few,' he said. *'Il est bien gentil.'*

We walked across the dried-up fields full of grasshoppers. I had met M. Ablard once or twice, his wife never. The house was silent and shuttered, the yard shimmered in the heat. I called, *'Il y a quelqu'un?'* and heard a voice inside. We waited under the porch which was mercifully shaded by trees. M. Ablard staggered out closing the door behind him, not so much to keep us out as to keep out the fierce heat, or perhaps both – I think he'd been having a late siesta. He was very gracious and told us to take whatever we wanted. No, he did not want any money. *'Pas du tout!'* His brown leathery face creased into a smile, he coughed horribly, re-lit a roll up and disappeared indoors.

The next day was market day and we left our gentle giant to heave the great cut stones into place and enjoy his radio. He was a fan of Radio Monte Carlo which I could barely endure for half an hour before asking him to switch it off. Apart from the distortion on his cement spattered transistor, Lulu singing 'Shout!' is not my idea of suitable background music on a still morning in high summer.

As soon as the wall was finished, M. Gibelou returned, and in two days the transformation was complete. Back and forth he went until all the top soil was pushed in close behind the wall. Next he transferred the remaining chalky soil into a gently sloping bank behind it. It was immensely skilful work. The digger was often at a crazy angle, and he would adjust the stabilisers and swivel his seat round and round, to control first the scoop and then the bulldozer. When he had finished, there was not a breezeblock to be seen and the wall looked as if it had always been there.

True to his word Raymond did come up to swim nearly every day. We bought a couple of umbrellas, for even though he would not arrive until about seven in the evening, once he was dry he always sought the shade. We were sipping an aperitif one evening when I noticed a strange little bird on the telephone wire.

'*C'est quoi, ça?*' Mike demanded, glancing up. Raymond got up to look.

'*C'est un oiseau bleu,*' he pronounced solemnly, shading his eyes. We laughed. We could see that. It flew away and Raymond began to talk about the seriousness of '*la sécheresse*', the drought, and said that many young farmers who had large loans would go under. The bird flew back. It was a budgerigar. It did a few alarmed sideways sallies along the wires, a less than confident somersault, and dropped down onto the cement mixer which M. Duparcq had not yet taken away. I grabbed a few biscuit crumbs and he fed from my hand nervously then flew back up onto the wire. Raymond laughed and went to get changed. The bird was still there when he climbed up onto his tractor.

'You'll never catch it,' he said. 'And it won't last long with the kestrels about.' Then starting the engine he added, 'But if you do, we've got an old cage somewhere.'

The budgerigar was thirsty. He took little sipping dives into the pool and then, perched once more on the cement mixer, allowed Mike to pick him up. We put him gently in a bucket with some food and a net over the top and took him down later to the farm. Claudette hunted out the old cage and everyone came to look.

'*Il va languir seul,*' said Grandpa. 'They pine alone.' There wasn't much I could do about that. And in any case someone might report him missing and I would have to hand him back. For days he was silent. But one morning about a week later he began to chatter and trill and we became very used to our unexpected guest. We christened him Biggles as we reckoned that with so many predators around he had been pretty intrepid to fly abroad. And no one claimed him.

The heatwave continued, day after day of fierce, unbroken sunshine. The kitchen, still flat packed, reproached us. I cooled my wrists under what should have been cold, but was, in fact, lukewarm water coming straight out of the ground and, shielding my eyes against the light, left the cool of the house for the oven outside. I suddenly thought of those television images of African women walking for hours with water pots on their heads. I had seen but not, until that moment, understood.

We eventually decided that it was no use waiting for the weather to change and our friend Hugh, who had offered to be in charge of the kitchen conversion, was anxious to get started. One more visit to *Electricité de France* and we were upgraded to a higher wattage. We would have liked to have power points put in every room but that would have to await more funds. Out went the detested old gas cooker, and our new kitchen corner in the big living room began to take shape. M. Albert came to relieve our lovely, hand-cut, granite arch in the corridor of the ancient gas geyser he had so unfortunately sited many years before. I was surprised when he proposed to put the new electrically heated water cylinder directly above the refrigerator in the *chai* but it was completely different from my eiderdown jacketed cylinder in London which heats an airing cupboard. This gleaming enamelled tank was not even warm to the touch. By midday it was too hot to work even indoors and the pool was in constant use. Raymond would come up every evening but Claudette, ever practical, had decided that the best way to learn to swim was to enlist professional help. Her second cousin Roland and his wife Nicole, who is also a teacher of gymnastics, soon started a school of swimming. Several times a week they would come with their three beautiful children. They would patiently coach the beginners and then, as we lay exhausted, would put us all to shame, diving and weaving through the water with grace and style. Our younger son Matthew arrived from London. He found a few lengths quite taxing to begin with but soon improved, and astonished us by spending hours at the typewriter, a side of him we had never seen before. We bought more chairs and tables to accommodate the alfresco meals we enjoyed. We were fifteen around the pool for supper one evening, including Granny and Grandpa who had come to see what was going on. I made the salads and provided the cheeses. Roland brought freshly slaughtered veal to barbecue. Hugh, his wife Sally and his children arrived with chocolate mousse and lemon tart and Claudette brought up a couple of kilos of strawberries. I watched the children laughing and talking a mixture of English and French, and any last, lingering doubts about the wisdom of having a pool vanished with the smoke from the barbecue, as it drifted upwards in the still evening air.

8

Sitting with my feet in the pool I watch as the maize in the great field is cut a month early. This wonderful summer for swimmers has been a disaster for many farmers. What promised in late spring to be a bumper crop will now yield no fat, golden cobs but must be crunched and munched into silage. The new machines on loan from the farmers' *Coopérative*, as brightly coloured as children's toys, toil up and down, whining like angry and persistent insects. The trailer lorry moves parallel with, but just slightly ahead of the combine, catching the shreds like breakfast cereal, which spout forth in a high sweeping arc. Fortunately what little wind there is blows from the north-west so none of it will be carried as far as the pool.

Only the top leaves of the maize are still green. The flowers droop like desiccated tassels and, as the rows are cut, brown dry tunnels are left behind. Up come the harvesters again. Dust swirls as they turn in formation and the diminishing square of maize in the middle of the field is eaten up five rows at a time by the silver bullet-like cutters on the front of the combine. The trailer full, it moves off with its pea-green load. There is a moment of silence until Raymond trundles across the field on his old tractor with a battered high-sided iron trailer. The combine costs too much to be left idle while the smart lorry is emptied. They begin again.

My eldest son Adam arrived with his lady Caz. I fondly watched the mother-to-be of my first grandchild swimming lazily in the pool. As I listened to them happily talking bird nonsense to Biggles, and making plans to return as a family the following summer, the prospect of yet another generation to enjoy Bel-Air gave me great happiness.

The wall now finished, we went to the nursery for plants to make a screen along the top of the bank. Laurels, quick growing and evergreen, seemed an obvious choice but, not wanting a uniform row, I interspersed them with a *vibernum tinus* and an *elaeagnus ebbengei*, a shrub with which I was unfamiliar. The nurseryman pointed out the attractive leaves which were glossy green above but silver underneath. I did not discover until several years later that in late September, it bears tiny hidden white flowers which fill the air with perfume. I bought a dwarf conifer. I also couldn't resist a magnificent pampas grass but neither could I make up my mind exactly where to put it. For weeks it sat in its container as we moved it from one place to another.

M. Duparcq returned to pave the rough concrete surround of the pool with a smooth crazy paving called locally *pierres d'Allemagne*. I have no idea if they do in fact come from Germany but the irregularly shaped pieces contain intriguing fossils, and they were considerably cheaper than more conventional tiles. My ambition was to somehow blend this blue rectangle into the garden and these stones, when grouted with the same cream cement as the wall, made a harmonious whole.

71

Claudette came up to invite us for Sunday lunch. She had the kind of gleam in her eye that means one of her specials. As usual we arrived promptly at midday. We were pleased to see Roland's father, *l'ancien inseminateur* turned beekeeper, and his brother, *l'ancien garagiste*, and their wives. Aperitifs were unusually prolonged because Houpette, Philippe's hunting dog, had disappeared and Willy, 'le Yorkshire' was also missing. Exactly who had led whom astray was a matter of heated debate, but it was clear that there was no question of lunch until the miscreants were caught, especially Willy. The hunting dog, it was thought, might find her own way home.

The next guests to arrive, on learning the news, disappeared again in all directions. There were phonecalls, much throwing up of arms and recriminations. Willy 'le Yorkshire' had been a present to Véronique, the daughter of the house, from her new fiancé, Jean-Michel, a striking young man with black hair and deep set eyes of a startling blue. At last Véronique returned with a disgusting Willy – muddy, fur tangled and unrepentant. Everyone yelled at him. Apparently he was up at Bel-Air. I was only thankful he hadn't fallen in the pool. Houpette slunk into the courtyard a few moments later to be given a good roar at by Grandpa and, at last, we sat down to lunch at an unheard of 1.30 p.m. The weeks of continuous heatwave had made even soup redundant. We began with a huge platter of cold fresh salmon, large prawns, and both tomatoes and eggs *farcies*. The dish was decorated with wedges of lemons and it was these which caused the most comment.

'*Ah! le vrai goût du citron*,' enthused the wife of *le garagiste*, for these lemons had a stronger, sharper and more perfumed taste. They had been picked but an hour before from Claudette's own tree. It was now so large that the tub in which it grew had been mounted on wheels to push it indoors when there was the slightest danger of frost – not that anyone was thinking about frost as, outside, the thermometer rose steadily in the baking courtyard. We drank a very delicious Sancerre with the fish and then my eyes brightened as Raymond put a bottle of *Vieux Cahors* on the table. It is my favourite of all wines but one glass is all I can manage. Perhaps two.

'What year is it?' I asked. He shrugged.

'The label has fallen off,' he said, 'but it's about twenty-five years old.'

'*Plus!*' shouted Grandpa from the end of the table as Claudette carried in a steaming casserôle. I watched the beekeeper's face twitch in every mobile muscle as the first waft reached his wide nostrils. His fleshy lips quivered.

'*C'est fait avec des pruneaux!*' he breathed. 'Ah!'

'*Bien sûr*,' laughed Claudette, she knows his taste. This was a *civet de lièvre*, jugged hare, worthy of George Sand herself, with the added prunes which are so much a part of this region. More bread was cut to mop up the rich aromatic sauce, and various tales about the ravages of the drought were told. The beekeeper's wife complained that her husband was mad. He had been off to his hives in the hottest part of the day. '*Il est fou, lui*,' she cried. 'It's very dangerous.'

Her husband explained between mouthfuls that it was imperative to hose the hives. If they became too hot the bees would swarm, taking out the eggs and the queen to preserve them, and he would lose the lot.

The *civet* was repassed but we all knew that there was more to follow. The next course was *magret de canard*, fillet of duck breast cut into slices. This was served with celery hearts in a thin Bechamel sauce. Raymond opened a bottle of Burgundy and the *garagiste* and his wife told of their trip to Egypt that winter. Grandma looked doubtful. '*Mais ... vous avez bien mangé, là bas?*' she asked. Did you eat well?

'Oh ... *pas comme ici, mais ... c'est normal*,' conceded the *garagiste*. 'But me, I don't mind trying a different cuisine.' Grandma looked unconvinced and the beekeeper gave his brother a sceptical look.

'It's part of the fun of travelling,' laughed the *garagiste*'s wife. 'I love being retired,' she added. 'When we're at home I'm up at six to work in my garden and – best of all – there are no more meals at nine and ten at night – after his work was done.'

'*Qu'est ce-que vous voulez?*' said her husband. 'When someone needed their tractor urgently you had to carry on.' He smiled contentedly. 'Now we eat at seven and work in the garden afterwards.'

Raymond looked pensive. There is little chance of his being able to retire and he prefers not to think of the future.

We sat at the table until five o'clock finishing the meal with *Baba au Rhum*, one of Claudette's specialities, and strawberries. 'These will definitely be the last of the season,' she said. 'They are being eaten by a cloud of wasps.'

At six we all came up to Bel-Air. Some swam; others played *boule*. The *garagiste* and Raymond rode up in the old car hooting loudly. It is a 1929 Citroën which belongs to Grandpa. It was hidden from the Germans in the barn behind the church. There it stayed for the next forty years until Philippe and my son Matthew, then teenagers, discovered it, and begged the old man to take it out and put it into working order. The original tyres were pumped up and it was the *garagiste* who got it going. Now it only does short journeys but everyone vies to drive it. It has the original plate with Grandpa's name on the back and was, I imagine, the envy of all the young men of the district when new. Grandma once told me that she had several suitors when she was a girl, but that her brother had encouraged her to marry Grandpa, '*Parce que c'était lui qui avait une voiture!*' Because he was the one with the car.

At half past eight the other guests left for home and Raymond begged us to go down later '*pour finir une belle journée*' as he put it. He went off to muck out the cows, and Claudette to see to her ducks, chicken, turkey, guinea-fowl, rabbits and pigs, while we watered our parched garden.

Thanks to M. Albert's thoughtful suggestion, a length of hose had been laid under the pool terrace while it was under construction. Connecting joints had been fitted and, once the main hose was attached, we could now easily water the far side of the meadow. We discussed the next project, which was to protect the pool from the east. I wasn't sure about another wall. We watered in our small laurels and moved the unfortunate pampas grass to yet another location.

At ten o'clock we were back at the farm, sitting outside in the courtyard. Claudette brought out a tureen of soup. It was the famous local garlic soup, *le tourin*, with which sleeping couples are surprised in the middle of the night, as were Philippe and Corinne on their wedding night.

But just who had they been planning to surprise tonight ... us?

Raymond grinned and nodded. 'We thought about it,' he said.

As we ate the soup together we reminisced about the first time they had initiated us into this ancient custom. We had awoken from a drunken slumber to find half the village in our bedroom and an extremely alcoholic party being prepared in the room next door. Raymond retold the tale with glee.

'*Oui, c'etait quelque chose* ... that was really something *et ... on a bien pensée pour ce soir,*' he said, '*mais ...*' he shrugged.

As it was on that night twelve years before, the moon was full, and I'm sure that it affects everyone but so, alas, does growing older. I have the feeling now that to bring *le tourin* is something that will be left for the young. We enjoyed the soup anyway, and lazily finished up some cold duck, as Claudette put jars and packages into bags for Philippe and Corinne to take home to Toulouse. Philippe works for a sugar company and seems happy enough but they come back almost every weekend and stock up. I didn't envy them the journey down that long, hot road but they seemed unconcerned as, with kisses all round, they climbed into their laden car, Corinne wearing only a sarong over her swimsuit. Véronique and Jean-Michel left too with a subdued Willy, washed and brushed and with his hair tied up in a ribbon. The old people went off to bed in their little house at the far end of the courtyard, and we sat talking quietly until Raymond's eyelids began to close.

We had six weeks of unbroken sunshine that first summer of the pool. Towards the end of August there was a sudden storm in the night and the first rain ran off the baked earth. The daytime temperature plummeted twenty-five degrees Fahrenheit. Raymond brought us a large sheet of plastic from Agrilot, the farmers' store, to cover the pool and conserve the heat. For two days we piled on our sweaters, but, as always, it warmed up again.

We found yet another site for the pampas grass, dug a hole and filled it with water. Two days later the water was still there. Clearly the pampas grass would not thrive on top of a rock, and we were extremely glad that we had not chosen that site for the pool. We made a trip to Albi to see the marvellous Toulouse Lautrec collection and, on the way back, saw the solution for a protective screen for the east side of the pool – not one, but a glorious hedge of pampas grasses. We finally planted the one we had, and were about to go to the nursery for more, when friends arrived from the Dordogne.

'We've got a huge pampas grass and we hate it,' they said. 'We'll dig it up and bring it over.'

The next week we all learned how razor sharp the leaves are as we divided the great clump and heeled it in. It has been a great success since then, providing an impenetrable wind shield and a row of spectacular plumes.

The balmy days of September with their golden light were with us, and at last we received the call we were hoping for. Our dear friend Tony was well enough and determined to travel, and would arrive with Nan in two days time. We went to Agen to meet the train. After we drove up the track to Bel-Air – only a year late, as he put it – Tony went off with Mike to open a bottle. Nan had a quiet weep in the garden at the sheer relief of a visit she had thought they would never make again. Sharing our house with friends is one of the real joys of Bel-Air, and finding that it is a special place for them too, is a bonus.

In spite his self description as a 'totterdemalion' Tony was, in fact, his usual lucid self, full of verbal sparkle. The only sign of his operation was a slightly drooping eyebrow which had, temporarily, to be taped up. He found this less tiresome when I told him that that was what strippers used to do with their boobs.

He and Nan were delighted with the pool, but the rest of the meadow, bare, brown and stony, was an eyesore. If we wanted anything resembling a lawn, we would have to prepare the ground.

We collected as many rakes as we could find and, on the morning we started work, Raymond drove by on his tractor. That evening he thoughtfully trundled up again with a small trailer and carted away all the stones. We raked and sieved until we were exhausted, then went to buy grass seed. We weighed and roughly measured out the amount for each square metre, and Nan and I sowed it by hand, trying to scatter the seed evenly. Each day we watered it gently and prayed that it would rain after we had left.

We swam until October, covering the pool each night, and taking Biggles indoors as it grew dark. We covered his cage with an old cotton skirt. The only trouble was that he would hear an early morning call from a bird outside and from underneath his frilly cover would chirp and trill very loudly from the kitchen table, waking everyone up.

My washing machine had also been making strange noises all that summer and now refused to work at all. It was, in any case, very old. I rang M. Albert.

'*Ma machine à laver, elle est morte,*' I said.

'*Ah, c'est triste. L'enterrement c'est quand?*' When is the funeral? he asked in his gentle voice. He promised to bring me a replacement but the days passed and nothing happened. Twice I rang and spoke to his wife.

'*Oh là! Il faut lui tirer les oreilles!*' she said, sympathetic to problems with the washing. I don't know whether she did pull his ears for me but, eventually, he arrived with a second-hand machine.

'Try this,' he said. 'It seems a pity to buy a new one when you will be leaving it to the mice in ten days.'

The hoses on our old machine had often been chewed through by hungry rodents during the winter. I started on the first of many loads of washing. He stayed long enough to make sure the machine was working properly and, before leaving, invited us to lunch on the following Sunday.

We had often had aperitifs *chez Albert* when we were planning another plumbing venture or paying a bill, but we had never eaten with them before. We arrived at midday, bearing the obligatory plant for Madame, and sat down with one Grandpa, two great Grandmas, Grandparents Albert, their two sons and their wives, and six grandchildren. We were made very welcome. Home-made aperitifs were followed by slices of saucisson made by Great Grandma, and crêpes filled with ham and mushroom in bechamel sauce. M. Albert then left the table to help cook and then *flamber* the tournedos. Great sizzling flames leapt from the grill and the children shouted with glee. We drank a simple wine – there was no *Vieux Cahors* – but we felt honoured to be included in such a family gathering. We talked about our plans to divide our *chai* and make half of it into a family bedroom, and the possibilities of moving our *cave*, and making an adjoining shower room.

'*C'est pas difficile,*' encouraged M. Albert. '*A l'année prochaine,*' we toasted, and to our hopes that we too would have a grandchild, when we next saw them.

It was time to begin closing the house. It always took

several days and this year there was the pool to attend to. We had cleared the terraces. The guest bedrooms were already full of plastic tables and chairs and umbrella stands. We made a last trip to M. Bourrière for advice on overwintering the pool. It was fairly simple and consisted of draining the pump and filter, and adding extra chlorine and an anti-freeze and anti-algae product. We bought a winter cover of very heavy-duty plastic. It had slots around the edge into which we pulled sausage-shaped tubes, which we then filled with water. They became so heavy there seemed little risk of even the most fearsome wind being able to lift the cover.

I had one more visit to make before we left for England. Anaïs, so much a part of the spirit of my house, lies buried with her son in the churchyard, high on the top of the hill. I was relieved to see that the houseleeks that I had planted on her grave the year before had not only survived the drought, but had begun to multiply. I planted a few more, tidied the weeds, and stood for a moment looking at the superb view. It is a place of great peace. On either side of her are imposing family tombs, highly decorated. Her simple grave with its covering of the fat, green rosettes of *semper vivum* is, in my opinion, the most beautiful.

9

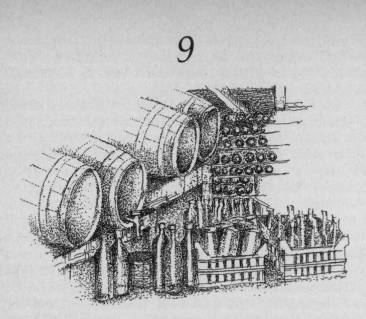

On the fifth of January my first grandchild, Thomas Joseph, was born. He was two weeks early, surprising us all – and very beautiful. My sister, an experienced grandmother, rang with salutary advice. 'Remember, he's not yours!' she said. The importance of this new life, and the love and security with which he was surrounded, contrasted horribly with the nightly television images. Distraught women and babies were suffering, on both sides, in the obscenity of the Gulf War. I could not bear to listen to the endless male chorusing of missile deployment, nor watch the grey-faced men in suits file in and out of conference chambers. I am not exactly a rabid feminist, but I became increasingly angry.

As if to soothe the insupportable, London was suddenly buried under a duvet of snow. The twigs in the garden were candy-flossed and still it fell, relentlessly, softening every urban angle. Concerts were cancelled and traffic noises were miraculously hushed, until the inevitable thaw turned the roads once again into black, tyre-gripping filth.

In early spring the advance copies of *A House in the Sunflowers* came thudding into the porch. I sat up in bed and read it from cover to cover and I couldn't wait to get back to France. We flew from Gatwick to Toulouse and then by a fluke – the train was late – caught an instant connection and managed to do the whole journey in three and a half hours. Although it was early April the weather was glorious, reaching eighty degrees by midday. Raymond came to meet us at our little station. Everyone was well, especially Grandpa who stomped in triumphantly from the fields with a kilo of *mousserons*, a tiny wild mushroom that grows in a ring. Grandma too seemed in fine form and a summer diamond wedding more and more likely. But there were other celebrations in the air.

'Come and look,' said a smiling Claudette. She was preparing a cradle. It was the very same one that she had slept in as a baby and had used for both Philippe and Véronique. She was re-covering it with new fabric for her first grandchild who would be born in a few weeks. But that was not all. Véronique, who in those early days when we had first begun work on our derelict house had been a plump little ten-year-old, was to be married at the end of August. This was going to be a very full summer.

The next day we had hardly got the plastic covers off all the furniture before Raymond rang up. *'Bonjour.'*

'Bonjour.'

'Ça va?'

'Oui – ça va. Il y a quelque chose?'

There was a pause. *'C'est-à-dire ... '* Raymond always begins this way when he wants a hand with something. But in fact we were more than ready to go down to the farm the following day to help with the bottling of two hundred and fifty litres of wine. The best quality red from the local *Cave des Sept Monts*, it had been put into the famous old oak barrel with the taste of *Vieux Cahors* four years earlier; each year since then it had been taken out, the barrel washed, and the wine replaced after a careful tasting.

We arrived the next morning to find the scene of activity, not as we had expected in the long, narrow wine-scented *cave* which runs underneath the full length of the farmhouse, but outside in front of the old barn. The lemon tree pushed out to enjoy the sun was ablaze with fruit. In front of the tree, eleven large dustbins stood in a very straight line. A couple of dozen crates were lined opposite them. In between was a row of chairs. The reason for the somewhat formal organisation was soon apparent as Jean-Michel, the son-in-law to be, strode round the corner wearing a large plastic apron and carrying a selection of long handled bottle brushes.

'*Bonjour tout le monde,*' he grinned. We had already noticed that there is nothing he enjoys more than setting up a new system. We wondered idly how this would go down with Grandma whose answer to many of my queries in the past was always '*c'est notre système,*' but she seemed to be content.

The bins were full of dusty bottles in soak. 'I'm afraid we just haven't got round to washing them yet,' laughed Claudette. They had to be rinsed inside and out, scrubbed, and then filled with a sterilising liquid, before being upturned and left to dry. With more than three hundred and fifty bottles to do it took all morning. After lunch we went to taste the wine. Was it, after all, worth bottling? We agreed that it was even better than the last lot. The next day we spent the morning crouched in the *cave* in our primitive assembly line. Not for Jean-Michel, Grandma's old system of lining the bottles up on unsteady planks on the beaten earth floor to be corked. '*Mais non! Mais non!* We'll put them straight into the crates,' he announced. 'It will save hours!' He was absolutely right. It was my job to fill each bottle from the great barrel. The others worked so fast that I didn't bother to turn off the tap between each bottle. I found my own '*système*' to change hands and niftily place each succeeding bottle under the tap only spilling, I thought, the occasional drop. But when I took off my socks that night there was an overpowering smell of red wine.

We left our share of the bottles in Raymond's *cave* because we were in the process of deciding to change the location of our own. When we had first begun our modest collection of wine, supervised and encouraged by Raymond, we had used one of the outside former pigsties as he had suggested. It faced north, and in it we had reassembled every old wine rack that we could find and fixed them to the uneven walls. It had served us well. But now we had plans to make our *chai* into a family bedroom and the wine store, being next door, would make a very convenient shower room.

During the winter we had drawn many plans. A *chai* is a small barn attached to the house, usually north-facing as it replaces a *cave* underground. It is left earth-floored and it is used for storing the wine, and anything else which needs to be kept as cool as possible. The highest wall in our *chai* adjoining the house is some twelve feet tall and reaches up into the attic. The roof then slopes on down dramatically to meet the outside wall which is only just over five feet high.

When we first saw Bel-Air on that hazy, hot day in the summer of 1976, it was along the length of this low wall that the original wine barrels, by then sadly rotted, had rested. Eight massive *barriques*, they were propped up on heavy, rough timbers. The *chai* at that time had been stuffed with cobwebbed museum pieces of farming equipment. During our first summers we were far too busy making the interior of the long derelict house habitable, to bother with the *chai*. When we did eventually begin to work on it we had our one and only real disaster. As we had carted out primitive winnowing machines, rakes, grinders, bed warmers and weighing machines and stored them in Raymond's barn, we had realised what a lovely space we now had. It was about seven metres by seven, the floor was beaten earth and the walls were a metre thick, and of rough, unplastered, beautiful stone, except for the high wall which had once been very crudely rendered with earth. The reason for this was, we guessed, that there were several rather large cracks in it. We decided that it might be a good idea to have just this wall cemented, at the same time as he did the floor.

Our friend, M. René, the elderly *maçon* who had already done a great deal of good work for us at very reasonable prices, wrote on a board on the high wall *CREPIS CE MUR* and we left that summer confident that this would be done. It took me several years to get over the trauma of opening the door of the *chai* on our next trip, to find all the beautiful stones covered with cement, and the high wall untouched, the board still on it. There was no possible way of changing it. It has occurred to me, over the years, to wonder whether in those intervening months, something, perhaps a broom, had fallen sideways over the written instructions, and it had looked like *PAS CE MUR*. I'll never know.

M. René had retired. We had found someone else to eventually '*crépis ce mur*' and the *chai* had now become a general junk room. With all that space, it was alarming how much rubbish accumulated. If we divided it in half, we now reasoned, we could still have an adequate store room, as well as our proposed family bedroom. We already had three bedrooms. This would make a fourth and we have never used the attic for accommodation. Bel-Air looks small from the outside but it is rather like the Tardis – deceptively large inside.

The sunshine continued. We arranged a rendezvous to introduce our gentle giant M. Duparcq to M. Albert. We decided that, rather than have two rooms with ceiling heights varying from twelve to five feet, we would divide the *chai* from east to west and use the lower end for the bedroom. The high wall would be more use for storage and, at the far end, M. Duparcq would build a separate, all important *cave* for our wine. We ran down our stock with pleasurable abandon, and carefully removed our remaining, dusty bottles from the ancient pigsty, storing them temporarily in our dark corridor.

While we were planning our new room, Claudette, as well as preparing for the new baby, had already begun to make a garland for the wedding still some four months ahead. It was to be a chandelier of paper roses, and was taking shape, suspended from a metal arm on a tall wooden stand in the inner room at the farm.

'Is the stand especially made for that?' I asked, imagining it to be a family heirloom.

'*Oui – mais c'est Jean-Michel qui l'a fait,*' said Claudette with obvious pleasure. In the coming years we found there were few things that Jean-Michel could not do, and his boundless self-confidence was seldom misplaced.

We worked in the garden every day. The grass we had sown made a green haze round the pool terrace. The laurels had all survived, and grown, and the pampas grasses were putting out new green fronds. We planted lavender and rosemary bushes. My bottlebrush shrub still looked as though it had not made up its mind, but the *lagerstroemia* that Ruth Thomas had given me, and that I had planted in a south-facing bed protected by a pine tree, was covered in bright green buds.

We were invited to the farm for Sunday lunch. Grandpa and Jean-Michel had been up early to fish in the lake by the château, and had returned triumphant with enough trout for everyone. We had the first and only meatless lunch we've ever eaten with the family. Soup was followed by a giant leek tart, and then the trout rolled in almonds, a salad and, finally, a flan, a stiff cream with caramel on top. A meal without meat was not to Raymond's taste but I had the impression that Claudette was eager to get back to her paper roses.

The brilliant spring sunshine had advanced all the crops

but, alas, the warmth did not last. An icy wind blew in from the north. It shrieked through the keyhole and, once again, we had to hang the blanket inside the front door. Raymond looked increasingly worried as the temperature dropped. There was no cloud cover at night and the plums, already set, were vulnerable. Each night the thermometer fell a little lower, until the dreaded minus six degrees was reached. The morning before we left, I understood why they use the word *grillé* for severe frost damage. The tender, light green buds on my *lagerstroemia* were now blackened and shrivelled, but more serious was the damage in the orchards and vineyards. Raymond dashed away the tears when we went down to commiserate. Some of the plums and vines would recover but, with the expenses of a wedding in the offing, it was not the moment for such a disaster. Grandma crept quietly into the kitchen. She shook her head.

'*Ah oui*,' she said. '*Quel drôle de métier.*' It's an odd way of making a living.

Back in London there had been no frost. My garden was a riot of spring flowers. The book came out and I began the usual round of promotional radio interviews. It was a somewhat *déjà vu* situation, Peter Mayle's second book having come out two weeks previously, but I was both surprised and pleased to receive many letters from people who seemed to prefer mine. I also got a good notice in *The Observer*.

Claudette rang to say that she too, was now a grandmother. A son, Clément, had been born to Corinne and Philippe. The next week she rang again to ask me if, in the summer, I would sing an Ave Maria at the wedding. I was happy to do so but wondered who would play for me. I found a lesser-known setting by Franz Abt that I had learned many years before, and which had a fairly simple accompaniment, and I started to polish it up.

Still in London, scouring the junk shops south of the river, we were collecting together odd bits of furniture which might eventually fit into the new room, and planning a route, when Mike went down with a viral infection of the ear called labarynthitis. The symptoms were most unpleasant; unless he was horizontal, it was as though he was continuously sea sick. Our efficient GP soon had the nausea under control, but the virus left him feeling very debilitated. I rushed up to SNCF in Piccadilly and was agreeably surprised to get a last minute booking to put the car on the train. So once again we left London and the next day were on the road from Brive at dawn and looking forward to a summer full of promise.

As we drove up the track to Bel-Air, Radio Monte Carlo was blasting out of our new family bedroom. M. Duparcq bent his head as he came out to greet us after, mercifully, switching it off. That apart, there were no disasters this time. Our *chai* was neatly divided. In the bedroom there was a new window space looking north up the meadow to the wood. A doorway had been cut leading out to the shower room to be, and M. Albert had already done the necessary plumbing, ready for us to choose a basin, shower and bidet. At the far end of the storage section was our new, purpose-built, wine store. Cool and dark, it only awaited racks and bottles.

M. Duparcq was busy finishing the bedroom ceiling. As it was directly under the roof tiles he had insulated it with glass fibre between the beams. Because of the lack of height at the lowest end, we had rejected an all-over false ceiling, and asked him instead if he could fill in between the curved and primitive beams with thin strips of tongued and grooved. This he had done and, although it looked handsome, it had clearly been a long and tedious job. But M. Duparcq is nothing if not stoical and, we were, of course, paying him by the hour.

It is always exciting to see a space transformed. I was already furnishing it in my mind's eye. The only object from the past still in the new bedroom was a tall, heavy but rickety cupboard which had always been there in one corner or another. It was black with age and dirt but it would never quite fall to pieces. When Mike suggested, on numerous occasions, that we might give it a helping hand, especially when he was dragging it into yet another position, I always insisted that one of these days I would strip it.

'Huh,' he would scoff, as we propped the corner up on a couple of bricks and leaned it at a crazy angle against the wall. But as far as I was concerned, it had always been in the *chai*, it had belonged to Anaïs, and I was keeping it.

One year we arrived to find that a feral cat had had four kittens in the bottom of it, and I surprised the skinny mother carrying in a baby rabbit. I pulled a face, imagining that I would eventually have to clear up the remains, but the kittens left nothing, not even a scrap of fur. They gradually got used to us, and although the mother cat would never come near, the kittens would approach for food, hissing and spitting all the while. I only managed to touch them when they had their heads in the bowl, and their tiny spines would quiver with fright. After three months they were healthy and strong and able to fend for themselves. There are always cats around and they do help to keep down the mice.

I took another look at the cupboard. It was very old but perhaps, with a bit of repairing, it might make a sort of wardrobe ... in any case I didn't think I could persuade my husband to move it yet again. It looked as though cupboard stripping, as well as Ave Marias, might be on my agenda for this summer. We left M. Duparcq and walked under the porch and into the house. There was the usual jug of flowers on the table, two jars of jam, and a bowl of eggs. Through the living room and into our bedroom, we pushed open the door to the south-facing rough terrace that I made so many years ago. It was covered in weeds as high as my waist. Startled lizards skidded off the stones. Insects buzzed in the heat. Shading our eyes we looked across the big field, *le grand champ* as Raymond always called it. It was a solid green, with thick stems and huge heart-shaped leaves and, here and there, flashes of a golden yellow that announced the beginning of the most spectacular crop of all – the sunflowers.

The grass on our lawns was three feet high and there were poppies round the pool and lace heads of cow parsley. The clematis, a Jackmanii, scrambled its purple stars to the roof. A rather weedy tree mallow had blossomed into a triumphant mass of pink. The small, bright green laurels had doubled in size and, behind them, a few roots of a yellow daisy that I had hurriedly heeled in before leaving the previous summer, had spread along like a bright golden-haired chorus line. The sun shone, the air was sweet, and it was very good to be home.

We unpacked the car, no kitchens this year, but plants for the garden, a tub of flat white paint for the new walls, and a travelling cot for Thomas Joseph. We hung up our clothes and, as always, I found garments in the wardrobe that I had quite forgotten I had. We began to carry out the garden furniture but then sat on it and simply admired the view. M. Duparcq finished for the day, bade us *'Bonsoir'* and bumped off down the track in his van. We dragged ourselves indoors, made the bed, the linen still smelling of the lavender I had put in the trunk last summer, and went down to the farm for supper, as we always do on our first night of the holiday.

The next day I saw Grandma as she walked slowly up through the fields. She quietly turned the corner by the pond and examined the sunflowers, as she passed along the track, stick in hand. She had come to inspect the garden. We did the tour together. She remembers everything that she planted for me in the early years, the climbing rose, the peony which I hardly ever see in bloom, and the tiny pine tree that she uprooted in the wood and brought down to us, now eight feet tall. We sat talking for a while about the coming diamond wedding celebrations.

'*Eh oui, c'est du travail,*' she said. It's a lot of work. '*Mais, pour soixante ans ...,*' she smiled almost disbelievingly. For sixty years – '*qu'est ce-que vous voulez ...*' And then she went off in a sort of dream. It was already very hot and, although she said she was quite capable of walking back again, when I announced my intention of going down to collect Biggles, who had been *en pension* at the farm during the winter, she gladly accepted a lift.

Once we had installed Biggles in his summer quarters outside the front door, and arranged my geraniums and other plants that Claudette had been overwintering around the top of the well, we were eager to get the cover off the pool and swim. We siphoned off a residue of water on the top of the winter cover, and then pulled out the stoppers on the heavy, water-filled, inner tubes. This was a job for bare feet, as we walked up and down on the tubes, trying to squeeze them flat. As the sun-warm water gushed out, there was much protesting from resident green tree frogs. They leapt in all directions when we began to pull the empty tubes out and roll them up.

As we turned back the cover, we stared in dismay. The pool was as green as the frogs. When we had left at the end of April, we had set the pump to filter the water for an hour, night and morning, as instructed. What had gone wrong? There had always been those who had warned us. 'Swimming pools ...' they had said ominously. 'Nothing but trouble!' Were we about to prove them right?

We telephoned Claudine. '*Oh là là!*' she said. 'But it's nothing to worry about. Leave the pump on all the time, add the shock treatment of chlorine and, in twenty-four hours, it will be perfect.'

We certainly hoped so. The family were arriving at the end of the week. We followed her instructions but, twenty-four hours later our pool was if anything, even greener. We rang again and, that afternoon, M. Bourrière's engineers came. They lifted up the green plastic lid and peered into the hole which housed the pump and the filter and, frequently, a large grass snake which seemed to like the warm, dark interior. The pump was fine, they said.

'We'll just put fresh sand in the filter.'

They seemed very confident. They hauled an industrial vacuum cleaner out of their van, and ran the lead back into the house. But when they tried to suction out the old sand their faces fell. The fine sand through which the water is filtered had become a solid block. They looked at one another. They pushed back their caps and scratched their heads. They had a go at tapping it with a hammer, but it was set like concrete.

'What could it be?' we asked.

They shrugged, mystified. The only thing they were sure about was that they would have to take the whole thing away. As they loaded the soldified filter onto their van we wondered how long we were going to be without a pool, but they promised to come straight back with a replacement. We weren't very pleased with the pool, but we certainly had no complaint about the service. An hour later back they came up the track. No sooner was the new filter in place than, to our great relief, the water began to turn paler and cloudy and, by morning we once again had a clear sparkling blue pool.

Later that day M. Bourrière phoned. He expressed his regrets, and asked us if we would take a sample of the water to Villeneuve for analysis and bring him the results. This we did, and learned the reason for our problem. The great drought of the previous year had necessitated the local water company extracting water from deeper and deeper underground. As a result, this water had contained more than the legal limit of chalk. Our house is not far as the crow flies or, presumably as the water pipes run, from the water tower. We were well aware that our old geyser had needed descaling every couple of years because of chalky water. The deep pumping of the previous summer had done the same for our filter in a few months. Fortunately most of the chalk had passed into the old filter and we have had no problems with the pool since then.

We spent the last few days before the family arrived in a whirlwind of house-cleaning, grass mowing and gardening. Raymond gallantly came up to help with his large cutter which he uses to clear the rows between the vines or the plum trees. It is very efficient, but I am constantly in danger of losing my toes, as I frantically guard some tender plant hidden in the grass edge. And of course once the grass is cut it still has to be raked and carted away. It was quite a relief to take a day off and drive to Toulouse to meet the plane and I was touched to hear my daughter-in-law say to her baby, as we drove home in the evening sunlight, 'Now look out here, Thomas, and you will see your mother's favourite view.'

Down on the farm, the tables were being laid for the diamond wedding celebration the following day. What had once been a primitive, open-sided barn next to the farmhouse had, over the years, been transformed into an outside dining room. The great diseased elms which had to be felled had been kept, seasoned, and used to remake the staircase which wound down from the attic. A smart false wooden ceiling covered the rough laths, the earth floor had been paved, and evidence of Claudette's passion was everywhere. Plumbago cascaded from its pot, bouganvilleas vied with tall chilean begonias, and there was every variety of geranium. I wasn't sure about the wooden light-fittings which were another of Jean-Michel's creations. He had fashioned them from old oxen yokes. Yet neither could

I imagine modern fittings being suitable, and Claudette was clearly delighted with them.

It was a beautiful morning. Apart from the family there were twenty-five guests, many of them over seventy. Six-week-old Clèment and six-month-old Thomas were introduced to everyone and behaved beautifully. Each guest had a heavy lined napkin, hand-embroidered with the grandparent's initials, which Grandma had made so many years ago as part of her trousseau. Large as pillow cases, they only came out for very special occasions. We had brought the old couple a pair of soft cushions for a present but at the last minute, I had found a very happy photograph of them both, taken the previous year at Philippe's wedding. I had it enlarged and stuck diamante all round the frame, and this seemed to delight Grandma. She stood it in a place of honour.

We began the meal with the most delicate consommé in which floated *perles du Japon* – a very romantic name for sago. Then Raymond's eyes lit up as the great platter of *foie gras entier* was passed down the table. He served with it a delicious white wine from Alsace. Next came a mixed *hors d'oeuvre* of artichoke hearts stuffed with crab, hard boiled eggs and prawns. I watched Grandma. Normally she scurries about helping Claudette with the serving but today, wearing a silk dress, her hair carefully styled, she was very much the guest of honour and she clearly enjoyed it, eating twice as much as she usually does.

Not one, but two different *civets* followed; one the usual hare, the other beef, and my favourite wine – a *Vieux Cahors* – to drink with them. The pace of the meal was leisurely. We had the afternoon before us. Clèment slept soundly and Thomas, after trying one or two mashed spoonfuls of various tastes, drank his milk and followed his example.

Grandpa reminisced with his old friend with whom he had been a prisoner of war in Germany for five years. As we helped to clear the table for the next course, the wives talked of hardships they had endured, as they tried to keep the work on the land going without their menfolk.

'*Ah oui,*' they nodded. '*C'était dur.*' It was tough.

Claudette carried in a dish of slices of *rôti de veau* with the ubiquitous *haricots verts*, and Raymond proudly served a '76 Pomerol which was greeted with much enthusiasm. Toasts were drunk to the old couple.

Grandma asked me to sing and I began with a song she taught me. '*Le Temps des Cerises*' – Cherry Time. I don't suppose Grandma knows or cares that it was written in 1866 by one Jean Baptiste Clément who, escaping from the defeat of the Commune, took refuge for a short while in London. He dedicated it to '*la vaillante citoyenne Louise*', who drove an ambulance in riot-torn Paris. All Grandma knows is that it is a song of love and nostalgia with a haunting melody. I then sang the song they all know and which reminds me of her – 'J'attendrai'. In all her sixty years of marriage the longest, I suspect, were with Claudette newly born, those five years that she spent waiting and wondering if Grandpa would ever come back from the prisoner-of-war camp in Germany.

10

Babies are the greatest time-wasters in the world but perhaps they simply give us an opportunity to marvel at the miracle of humanity. In the three weeks that Thomas was with us he ran our lives. Guests of his parents flew in for short breaks in their busy schedules. Adam's friend, Tom Harvey, was amazed to see that the rough barbecue they had built together ten years before was not only still standing but in constant use. We cooked trout stuffed with rosemary and garlic, kilos of sardines and large fat prawns. The young went separately to the market and, often disorganised, came home with double quantities of everything, especially oysters.

On the one occasion when they all dined out, Thomas refused to go to sleep. By nine-thirty I gave in, hauled him out of bed and into his pram. Down through the orchard we bumped, while he looked up in some bewilderment at the dark branches of each succeeding tree. To my relief, the great round eyes began to narrow. He held out to the last however, staring at me though two black slits until sleep finally won the battle.

July was wonderful, bright blue skies with the superb prospect down from the pool across a vast expanse of sunflowers to the woods and valley beyond.

'I couldn't have a better view if I were a millionaire,' said my contented husband.

When I was a child my father was often out of work and, to supplement the dole, my mother would sit up dressmaking half the night. On Fridays she would count out her money into Oxo tins labelled 'rent', 'coal' etc. On the rare occasions when we did have a holiday, we would stay in a terraced house near the railway line in Little-hampton, where the unlovely landlady would throw us out at ten in the morning. For our midday meal we looked for the cheapest café. I hated being poor and would escape into my fantasy of becoming a film star, Bette Davis being my idol. I imagined myself incredibly rich with, of course, a swimming pool, and the ultimate triumph, returning one day to Littlehampton to travel slowly down the main street in an enormous, bright pink, chauffeur-driven Cadillac. As I sat by my pool that summer with my family around me, I knew that there were other sorts of riches, and I wasn't too bothered about the Cadillac.

After they had all left and we were tidying up, Mike knocked the telephone onto the tiled floor with a crash. We were hardly surprised to find that it no longer worked and, later that afternoon, we went down to the farm to call the engineers. Raymond laughed. 'That won't do any good,' he said. That very morning, he told us, he had been coming along the road on his tractor when he saw his neighbouring farmer in a field at the bottom of our track. He had just finished loading his tallest trailer with five great rounds of straw.

'*Il a justement fini,*' began Raymond dramatically. He had clearly told and retold this tale all day. '*Et avec les cinq grandes boules de paille,'* Raymond did a vivid mime, *'il a commencé à tourner.'*

Approaching, Raymond had seen the coming disaster. The five great rounds of straw obscuring any view to the rear, the edge of the trailer just caught the telephone wire. Raymond had waved and shouted, but as with his own smouldering load one previous summer, he had found that communication with a distant tractor is easily misinterpreted. As his friend waved back assuming Raymond's gestures to be some ecstatic *'Bonjour'* on this lovely morning, not only did he snap the wire and pull down the pole, but the next three telephone poles went down like dominoes. Once it was all mended our telephone worked perfectly.

M. Duparcq returned to cut and cement a drainage channel all round the north side of the house. I knew it had to be done. When the *chai* was only used for wine, it hadn't mattered if the earth floor became damp when there were heavy rains. Now that we had had it divided and intended to tile the cement floor of what would be our new bedroom, a damp course of some kind was necessary. The long, steep slope of the roof made the water cascade down the roman tiles and fall in a curtain off the lower edge, and it had to run somewhere. The new cement channel would slope gently down to a soakaway past the house but ... it necessitated digging up a great many of Anaïs's roses.

I already knew that M. Duparcq's feeling for stones did not extend to plants, but he nodded patiently as I tried to explain that, if it were possible, I wanted to save the roses and replant them further back. The sweat ran off his face and down his long back as he dug them up. After a light pruning, I pushed the tangled old roots into buckets of water and stood them in the shade of the ash tree. We had a lucky escape this time from Radio Monte Carlo as the batteries on the transistor needed replacing. The only electric plug near where he was working being the one I used for the washing machine, we had almost continuous laundering for several days. Once replanted, the roses revived.

The diamond wedding over, the final plans for Véronique's wedding at the end of August began to take shape. Hundreds of paper roses were being made, and everyone sat down with Grandma and made a few more when they had a moment. There seemed to be cartons of them in every room. The great paper chandelier, festooned with ribbon and flowers, hung in the corridor, and mysterious packages arrived almost daily. Claudette still came to swim but she did not stay to gossip. Pre-wedding preparations were a serious business. The whole house was scrubbed and polished. Her garden was exceptionally well weeded. Two large square tubs, one on either side of the balcony where the bride and groom would stand for the photographs, were ablaze with scarlet and yellow canna lilies and zinnias. The barn facing the house, which like all barns holding a thousand farming necessities was usually a loosely organised muddle, was ruthlessly tidied. She was now trying to persuade Raymond that the courtyard itself needed to be resurfaced.

'Oh, regarde! C'est pas joli!' she cried.

Raymond huffed and puffed but, as usual, gave way. Then it was heated discussions about exactly what colour gravel to use with the tarmac. We made trips to the quarry and to different villages to compare one person's drive with another.

Véronique herself was deciding, among a million other things, on the music for the ceremony. I was rather alarmed when she brought me piano copies of 'Jesu Joy of Man's Desiring' for the entry of the bride, and the march from *Aida* for the final procession. I must have spent a small fortune on pianists in my time. I am a less than adequate accompanist – a solo pianist I certainly am not. And in any case what was I supposed to play them on? There was no organ in our tiny village church. I reckoned that getting through my Ave Maria would be a sufficient responsiblity.

Singers are like athletes and must go into training for a performance. As well as entertaining the cows with daily scales, I had found a slight and nervous accompanist who lived in Villeneuve and I would go to his odd, impersonal house once a week to sing. He was quite proficient although he made most of his money copying and scoring music. He seemed to enjoy my varied programme which always finished with the Ave Maria for the wedding. I said goodbye to him for the last time as my friend Christina, a marvellous accompanist, was due to arrive the next day with her husband, her son and my sofa.

The sofa, a handsome, iron-framed antique, covered in a William Morris fabric had been donated to Bel-Air by *les Fostaires* some years before. The only problem was how to get it to France. The prices quoted were astronomical. The previous year our friend Hugh had, with some difficulty, (as it was extremely heavy) put it on a trailer and taken it from Clapham to High Wycombe. He intended to include it in a load of his belongings for which he was hiring a van. His own furniture safely on board, he found he had underestimated both the amount of space he needed and the size of our sofa. It made the return journey to Clapham where it sat, disconsolately, in a spare room.

One day, after a session with Debussy, I was discussing its plight with Christina, a lady who likes solving problems, musical or otherwise. Later that evening her husband Marcus arrived with a tape measure. After about ten minutes he announced that, if he could saw off the feet, he was pretty sure he could get it into his Volvo. They would be happy to bring it to the house in the sunflowers, and then put back the feet.

Friends bearing a sofa was an offer I could not refuse but, on the day they were due to arrive, there was no sign of them. I was slightly worried that the weight of the sofa might not only have delayed them but actually caused it to fall through the floor of the Volvo. Also the last sunflowers were beginning to turn and, in a few days, the once golden field would be patched with brown. I was relieved when the following morning they telephoned and, within a couple of hours, we saw them bumping slowly up the wrong track to the house, one really only suitable for tractors and our own old 2CV. As they drew nearer I could see ten year old Samuel in the back of the Volvo sitting in state on my sofa.

'I think he'll quite miss it on the way home,' said Christina.

Once unloaded, the sofa went into the living room where it fitted perfectly. It joined the ancient sideboard and farm table which had belonged to Anaïs and looked as though it had always been there. The covering fabric in dark red and ochre was a very happy choice with the terracotta tiled floor.

Once out of the sofa, Samuel lived in the pool. One day we invited the Albert family up to swim. The great grandparents stayed at home but everyone else came. Mme Albert cannot swim but she enjoyed playing with her grandchildren in the shallow end. The three year old, safe in a ring, suddenly discovered how to propel herself along and, with her dummy in her mouth, chugged up and down the pool and refused to come out. Eventually they had had enough and we put all the tables end to end and rushed about for chairs. I had prepared a huge rice salad with prawns and we barbecued small lamb cutlets with rosemary. By now it was past nine o'clock and, their work finished for the day, Raymond and Claudette came up to join us all for *le dessert*.

My English friends are always amused to see me making bread pudding but I find that it is the only way to deal with the vast quantities of french bread that are too hard to eat.

Because the French bake twice a day, their bread is not intended to keep, and guests invariably come back from market with a gigantic loaf saying. 'I just bought this – it looked so delicious.'

This bread pudding was the deluxe version. Highly spiced, it was stuffed with every kind of dried fruit and topped with brown sugar and toasted almonds. Raymond rubbed his hands.

'*Ah c'est le pudding au pain!*' he exclaimed. The Alberts looked polite but sceptical until they tasted it. We served it with vanilla ice-cream and as always I wondered why the British can't make ice-cream. In my local French super-market I can buy a wonderful range – blackcurrant, coconut, mango, pistachio, apricot, dark, dark chocolate and creamy, real vanilla. Even the cheapest own brand has twice the flavour of British ice-cream, and is less expensive.

After supper, Samuel, who was once more in the pool, was persuaded to play for us. He hauled himself out, shook the water from his red hair, dried his hands and went to fetch his fiddle. He was already a student at the Guildhall, and would later win a violin scholarship to the City of London School. Extremely talented, he had a wonderfully matter-of-fact attitude to performing. We all sat spell-bound, especially the little Alberts, as he stood by the pool and began to play. The acoustics were amazing. The sound reverberated off the wall of the house and to add to the magic, as if on cue, an almost full moon came slowly up over the hill. Later, when everyone had gone, we sat looking at the stars and Samuel was excited to see his first satellites, moving steadily in the wide, dark and mysterious sky.

Meanwhile the wedding preparations were accelerating. The bride and groom were to have their respective stag and hen parties on the following Friday night.

'*C'est pour enterrer le vieux garçon et la vieille fille,*' laughed Claudette. As it happened it almost did bury the groom.

The next day Jean-Michel looked very woebegone. He held his head stiffly and at an odd angle but it was not, as one might reasonably have imagined, the result of too much drinking. For their celebration the men had gone to a pizzeria with a swimming pool and, in the resultant horseplay with his friends, he had injured his neck. The girls had chosen a more upmarket restaurant. '*C'était un joli cadre*,' said Véronique happily, while stirring something on the stove. '*On a mangé du poulet avec une très bonne sauce d'écrevisses.*'

It seemed that her husband to be hadn't felt too bad that night, as they had all met up at 5.30 a.m. and danced till dawn. Today however it was a different story. He had been to consult someone – not it appeared Madame Orlando – as a result of which Véronique was now preparing a special brew of twenty-five walnut leaves and one root of *mauve* – wild mallow. She then soaked a series of cloths in the mixture and applied them to the injured neck.

Jean-Michel is the youngest of five, the others all being girls. During the day one sister after another kept appearing to see how he was. They drove in and out of the courtyard which was still in the final stages of being re-surfaced. Claudette and Grandma were moving furniture. They were clearing the corridor and setting out decorated tables to display the wedding presents.

Grandpa had had enough. '*C'est pas un mariage – c'est un cirque!*' he yelled, stomping back to his house.

I learned that a certain Mlle Bruet, who lived in the next village, would bring her portable organ to play for me at the wedding. I decided that with so much going on, it was up to me to arrange a rehearsal. Christina, Samuel and I met her at the church. She was a rather timid young woman. She plugged in the organ. I gave her the music and waited. She looked at it for a long moment then played one note. I hesitated. 'Er – the introduction goes like this,' I said, humming the tune. I pointed to the music. She wore thick glasses and stared at the notes as if they were the first that she had ever seen. She then played, very slowly, my opening phrase. I tried again. 'That's my line,' I said. 'You play the accompaniment underneath.' I smiled encouragingly, already knowing that I was in deep trouble.

She sighed. 'I only play the top line,' she said, 'with one hand.'

Christina and I looked at one another. There was a long silence.

'Would you mind – would you allow my friend to play for me?' I asked.

'*Bien sûr,*' she said. She practically fled from the organ while Christina couldn't wait to get her hands on the keyboard.

'Are you quite sure you don't mind?' we asked. It was, after all, her organ.

'*Pas du tout!*' To my great relief she genuinely appeared not to mind at all. We went through the Ave Maria. Unfortunately there was no possibility of Christina being able to play for the actual wedding as they were leaving the following day. We rushed back to the house for our cassette recorder and her husband Marcus's assistance. Then we realised that the organ was laid on a shelf next to the only electric socket in the church. Suspecting that the electricity supply to the church might well also be on *tarif primitif*, I couldn't risk blowing the fuse by using an adaptor.

The nearest house to the church was only used at weekends. Fortunately this was a Saturday. Rosaleen was watering her plants. '*Pas de problème,*' she smiled. '*Entrez, entrez.*'

But of course, there was a problem. The lead wasn't long enough and she didn't have an extension lead. Another journey through the village and up the track to Bel-Air and at last, we were ready to record. The shelf on which the organ was placed being high on the wall, it was necessary to play standing up, but nothing daunts Christina. Finding that on one side of the organ was a sliding volume control she enlisted Samuel's help. Bending her knees to indicate a crescendo and raising them again for a diminuendo, while Samuel pushed the knob back and forth, she played my accompaniment for my Ave Maria. She also very kindly recorded for me the other two pieces of music that Véronique had requested. Bach and Verdi were saved from being ill-used by me. Of course – it could have been even worse – they could have been left to Mlle Bruet!

11

When Philippe had been married we had only been on the periphery of the preparations. For this, the wedding of Véronique and Jean-Michel, we were completely involved. To decorate both the church and the *salle de réception* it is traditional to use wild asparagus fern, but the problem is that its whereabouts are a closely guarded secret. Not, as one might imagine, because there are so many weddings, but because the asparagus itself can be sold at market. Sadly, none grew anywhere on Raymond's land. Mike, who that morning had just finished varnishing the parking signs for the guest's cars, went off with Raymond to find some.

I imagine that Raymond had made some preliminary enquiries at farmers' reunions and they had to drive some distance. The chosen farmer, before taking them to his source, made them swear to secrecy. Although very sympathetic to weddings he was equally unwilling to lose any part of his livelihood. While Mike and Raymond bumped over a field to load our car with the long and feathery, but surprisingly prickly fronds, and bring them back to the farm to be decorated with the paper roses, I was sent to market to buy kilometres of pink and white ribbon. We cut it into strips and curled them with the back of the scissorblades.

We finished this task as a whole team of people arrived. Great branches of box were unloaded in the courtyard. They were to be cut into enough small pieces to fill several dustbins. Chairs and secateurs were provided. Imelda, a childhood friend of Claudette, had come from Paris with Robert, her husband. Staunch family friends, they often combine a holiday with help for various harvests. Sturdy and excited neighbours in sun hats and pinafores brought children to help and Grandma supervised the whole affair.

It was very hot and sultry. Jean-Michel, happily recovered – the poultice must have been effective – shinned up and down ladders decorating the outside barn, where they would later set up the bar. The old car was to be exhibited. It was cleaned and polished and adorned with streamers. In the afternoon, we, the team, which now also included the man who normally comes to do the muck spreading, went off in a convoy some five kilometres to another village where the *salle municipale* had been hired for the *grand repas*. It was a larger room than the Restaurant Palissy but less appealing, and we spent hours covering the bare walls. Jean-Michel's sisters and Philippe's mother-in-law were dab hands at twisting the asparagus fern to join it into continuous lengths. We then added the curled ribbons and paper roses and looped these garlands along the length of the room. Philippe arrived with a pump to inflate dozens of balloons and worked like a demon. There was no sign of the bride. She was, apparently, in Agen, *chez la couturière*. It was certainly a full-scale production.

While we decorated the hall, Mike and Raymond had been off on another quest, this time for juniper trees. They had found some promising looking specimens on a sloping hillside, separated from the road by a field of tobacco, in the process of being harvested.

'I can't give you permission to cut those trees,' said *le patron* when they enquired. 'I don't own the land. But I'm packing up in a few minutes and if you'd like to follow me I'll show you where you can help yourselves.'

He took them to a small wood of junipers near to an abandoned farmhouse, where the old man had died and the whole property was apparently in dispute.

'That's the way it's been for over a year now,' grinned the farmer. 'And until they sort it out you can take as many trees as you want.' They chose the eight most handsome, so tall they hung out of the back of the car. The first two they delivered to us at the *salle* to be trimmed with yet more paper roses. The others were for the doors of the church, the *Mairie* and the entrance to the farm. These delivered they then set to work to wash out 200 plastic bottles to hold the punch which Philippe had made the night before.

Véronique's ambitions for music for the wedding grew daily. Thanks to Christina we already had the entrance and exit music organised and, thank heaven, the accompaniment for my Ave Maria. Now I learned that a cousin from Bordeaux was going to sing another Ave Maria. Who was going to play for him? Mlle Bruet apparently. I said nothing but wished him luck.

Next Véronique returned from Agen with tapes for interludes of music during the service. I was pleased to see she wanted a Vivaldi Gloria but not so sure about the suitability of her next choice – the *Dies Irae*! I hoped I could manage to keep it all running smoothly. The afternoon before the wedding we had a rehearsal in the church. Each separate piece was recorded on a different tape to avoid having to wind on. This was kindly done for me by Nicole, our erstwhile swimming instructor. Mme Barrou had been up early and picked armfuls of marguerites. She had arranged them in vases the length of the church, turning all their faces to the altar. The musty building was filled with their freshness. At the front of the church are the oldest chairs which have the initials of the original occupants written in brass studs on the top. I looked down the line and saw A.C., Anaïs Costes. In this small, plain church I sat for a few moments in Anaïs's chair, and felt strangely moved.

The great day arrived. Véronique began her final countdown. At the hairdresser at seven, she next visited the dentist for a special nuptial clean and polish, before going on to the beautician for the customary professional make-up. The morning was hot but overcast. There was no wind. Claudette brought out the great paper chandelier that she had spent so many hours making, and hung it over the balcony. There was some initial alarm as to exactly who had the keys to the church. Raymond ran in and out anxiously. They were eventually found, and we were able to open up, set up the tapes and have a last-minute run through. The young men were still busy putting the final touches to a triumphal arch which stretched over the juniper trees at the bottom of the drive. The initials of the bride and groom were on either side of a heart, resplendent with yet more paper roses; no wonder we had had to make so many!

There was a moment of panic as the refrigerated lorry arrived. It was driven by Daniel who worked for a cheese firm, and would lend it for such an occasion, to throb away on the edge of the courtyard as an extra refrigerator. Would it pass underneath the arch? *'Doucement!'* yelled everyone as it inched through. Last of all a green pathway was laid with the thousands of pieces of cut box tree. It stretched from the door of the house across the courtyard down the long drive, under the archway and along the village street to first the church and then on to the *Mairie.* Total strangers passing through the village slowed down, leaning out of their cars to look.

The newly resurfaced courtyard was bright with tables

and umbrellas. Jean-Michel's mother arrived with great trays of homemade pizza. His sisters and various neighbours scurried about, filling rows of small dishes with nuts and nibbles, and the crates of punch were brought out from the *cave* and loaded into the refrigerated van. Every minute excited guests arrived very conscious of wearing their best clothes. Children jumped up and down and there was a great deal of kissing. Cars were directed to the car park before being decorated. People looked at their watches. At last all eyes were turned to the flight of steps, cameras clicked and the bride emerged.

It was hard to realise that this was the same little, plump, rosy cheeked ten year old who had once helped me clean my derelict ruin, and giggled over my dictation mistakes. She looked stunning. There was not the slightest trace of nervousness. Her dress was in satin with a long train, the low cut bodice heavily beaded, as was the hem. The short sleeves were puffed and ruched, but most distinctive was the hat. It was a tiny satin boater worn perched forward on her head with the brim curved up at each side. At the back was a huge tulle bow with floating ends which hung down to join the train. She looked as though she ought to ride off side-saddle on a white stallion holding the reins in her ruched and beaded satin-gloved hands. However, she was, of course, to walk – and quite a distance – and she began immediately to instruct the children how to carry her train before she started to descend the steps.

At that moment an anxious Jean-Michel arrived wearing a short black jacket and dark trousers with a very faint stripe. He gave the bride one swift approving nod and immediately ran up the steps to help with the train before inspecting the last minute arrangements of food and drink. Raymond came dashing out looking at his watch and Véronique, with the children adjusting the train, positioned herself on his arm and everyone fell into step behind. As they walked down through the village to the *Mairie* along their box-covered green route, followed by the excited procession, we left for their next entry as a married couple after the civil ceremony. I would like to have seen Raymond's face as they were married by the unpopular Mayor but I was waiting in the church – my finger on the button. The same cherubic old priest that had married Philippe and Corinne was to officiate and he said blithely that he would cue me for the musical excerpts.

'I will nod for you to begin Madame, *comme ça*,' he said. 'And raise my hand for you to fade out.'

How simple. I wondered how many couples he had married in his long career.

'Too many to count but each one brings me joy,' he smiled.

Two delicate old chairs which had belonged to Véronique's great grandparents were placed in front of the altar, facing the congregation, as the couple would be seated for most of the ceremony. Mike, positioned at the door, waved, there was a flurry of latecomers into the tiny packed church, I switched on the first tape and to the strains of Jesu Joy of Man's desiring, in they came. I hardly took in the service, I was so preoccupied with the music. The cousin from Bordeaux had a pleasant voice but was hardly helped by one-handed Mlle Bruet, droning away, often several bars behind him. As the service progressed people jostled for position with cameras but the little curé was unruffled. The introduction to my Ave Maria being only two bars long, I had to switch it on, and then move pretty fast into place. I actually sang rather well, the acoustics were good and Christina's sure accompaniment helped. But I was in such a hurry to get back to my music station for the next tape that, on the last Amen, I sang what must have been the worst note of my entire career, so I was astonished when the whole church burst into applause. And of course, that note is for ever preserved on the family video – no chance of a re-record.

The curé gave a short and moving homily about both the solemnity and the joy of the occasion '*au milieu de vous et devant Dieu*', and, the service over, to the march from *Aida* we followed the radiant couple. We crowded out of the tiny church, leaving yet more photographs to be taken at the door between the festooned junipers. Mike and I drove back to the farm, taking a handicapped relative, and so were able to see the bride and groom process once more up the green box pathway to the courtyard, followed by a great excited crowd. It was all kisses and congratulations and choosing of tables to enjoy the food and *le vin d'honneur*. Everyone was very hungry, there were delicious things to eat, and no-one really noticed that the light had faded and a little breeze was riffling through the umbrellas and beginning to swing the decorations.

Suddenly Véronique looked southwards and gave a cry. The sky was changing fast. An ominous, dark grey funnel was moving towards us at speed. With shouts of '*Orage!*' and '*Oh là là!*' all the previous organisation went into rapid reverse. Within minutes, umbrellas were folded and lifted out of tables. Trays of food and wine glasses with chairs and tables were dragged frantically under the cover of the two open barns on either side of the courtyard. In the midst of all the scrambling panic, I saw Claudette dash up onto the balcony, her dress whipped by the wind, to rescue her precious paper chandelier. She struggled for a moment but then managed to untie it and, holding it high in front of her, for it was almost as tall as she was, she raced for cover.

For the past month rain had been badly needed but, as it lashed down into the courtyard, making a swirling stream which washed away the carefully laid path of green box, the wedding crowd stood damply in their opposite shelters shaking their heads and throwing up their hands in disgust at such terrible timing. The temperature dropped and dropped, but miraculously, Véronique kept smiling. She and Claudette brought out a selection of cardigans and

111

jackets to protect flimsily clad shoulders. It rained hard for almost an hour but as soon as the rain eased the bride tripped from one side of the glistening courtyard to the other, greeting her guests with her train looped up on one arm. It was as good an example of 'the show must go on' as I'll ever see. But of course, farmers are ever philosophical about the weather and she is a farmer's daughter. Alas, there was no dancing as planned, the barns were too crowded, but the food and wine soon disappeared. By six o'clock the crowd had thinned and Mike and I were able to slip away and get our heads down for a couple of hours before *le grand repas*.

By late evening the storm had moved away and our endless convoy of cars passed beneath a serene sky washed with rose-edged clouds, to arrive at the decorated *salle*. The room looked very festive and we, the team, congratulated ourselves. It was clear that, safe from anything the weather could do, the bride and groom, still wearing their wedding clothes, were determined to enjoy themselves. The disco was set up by a professional *animateur*. My heart sank for they can be tedious, especially at village fêtes where they tend to keep up a continuous, loud stream of nonsensical chat. However, animated he certainly was, a sweet-faced and tireless young man who, as well as organising the toasts, the music and the dancing kept the children happy with crazy games.

One look at the menu and we knew we were in for a treat. We began with one of Grandpa's favourites, *salade Quercynoise*, a green salad sprinkled with small pieces of duck breast and gizzards, air-cured ham and walnuts. After that we were served salmon in a champagne sauce. At this stage there was a choice of wines; a *rosé* from our local *cave des Sept Monts* which is very good, a *Côte de Duras*, and a *Sauvignon*. With the *plat de résistance*, the ever popular *filet de boeuf* in the famous *sauce Périgueux*, we drank a *Bordeaux Château La Croix* '86. The beef was superb. I imagine

Claudette had chosen it again. The service was very slow and there was dancing in between each course and this time – sciatica free – I was able to join them. Everyone danced, the old and the very young. A long time after the beef came roasted quail with raisins and great dishes of *pommes forestières* – potatoes sautéed with wild mushrooms, garlic and parsley. I was amused to see the simple green salad which followed described on the menu as *'boulevard des escargots.'* Not a title which would happily translate.

The children played games for prizes while the cheese was passed and it was midnight before we reached the dessert and yet more young guests arrived. First we were served fruit salad in liqueur and then the wedding cake was carried in. It was not profiteroles this time but *'Un Moulin des Amoureux.'* It was a windmill with a miniature bride and groom in a very dangerous position were the sails ever to turn. The whole thing was made of biscuit and crisp caramel. The children gathered round with 'oohs' and 'aahs' licking their lips for the first taste. It was more like confectionery than a cake and must have taken hours to pipe all the sugar. It seemed a shame to destroy it but it got smaller and smaller as the evening wore on.

The *animateur* had a super microphone and with several glasses of good wine inside me and no tape to worry about I enjoyed singing unaccompanied. I had been practising, with the cows for audience, Marguerite Monnot's *'Hymne à l'amour'* and it seemed appropriate – with wonderful words by, of course, Piaf herself. We danced not quite until dawn, but until we were exhausted and left the young ones to it. The bride and groom would get little sleep as they would be woken up again almost as soon as they got to bed with the famous tureen of garlic soup, as a starter to the next party.

But my fondest memory of the whole affair is of Véronique the following day. There were many sore heads, including the new husband Jean-Michel, who retired to bed after the midday meal of leftovers, which we ate in the courtyard. But the *salle* had to be cleared. That, apparently, was part of the deal. So, led by the bride, off we went, an army of us, with plastic sacks, dustbins and brooms to the scene of the revelry of the previous night.

Down came the garlands, the balloons, the ribbons and the paper roses. The tablecloths were folded and the tables too. Chairs were stacked high against the walls and Véronique, in tee-shirt and faded leggings, swept the floor. Her young face bare of make-up, she looked like a very tired, but utterly contented, child. As though all her young life had been a preparation for this, she had a quiet confidence that she had chosen wisely and that it was now up to her and Jean-Michel to carry on the traditions and responsibilities of working the land. We collected up our laden dustbins. Would the decorations be stored somewhere for another party? I didn't know. The hall was bare again. As we filed out, and closed and locked the door, only the junipers, on either side of the porch, were left as a souvenir of *un temps de bonheur* – a time of great happiness.

12

Two days later the publicity department of Virgin Publishing rang to say that *Country Homes and Interiors* wanted to do a feature about Bel-Air and were sending a photographer. He was on his way. When would he or she arrive? Probably in a couple of days. We looked at each other in dismay. Of course it was good for the book, but for the last few weeks we'd hardly had time to look at the house, let alone spruce it up.

'Don't worry,' said Marie, the publicity girl. 'They don't want anything changed. They want it just as it is.'

I looked at the cobwebs in the corners, the dead horseflies on the window-sill, the dust on the mirrors, the paint flaking off the bedroom wall, and the little tin lids of mouse poison in the spare bedrooms and laughed. And so began the most thorough cleaning that Bel-Air has ever had, or is ever likely to have. Not that I am sluttish, you understand, but there are always more interesting things to do here than housework.

The interior of our country home began to gleam. Windows were supercleaned. Mirrors shone. Tiles were polished and the cupboards and chests now shone with scented beeswax. The assortment of Victorian china, none of it matching, which hangs on the dresser was plunged into soap suds. The wide open hearth was swept more scrupulously than ever before and all the soot was brushed off the fire back so that the design of two medieval grape-carriers could be seen. Plates on the walls were taken down and long-dead creatures removed from the rims. Rugs were beaten, frayed ends cut off. Beams were dusted, the porch was swept. Even Biggles got his cage spring-cleaned.

Claudette was amused. 'I'll lend you some extra geraniums for the porch,' she said. As I filled the bedrooms with vases of flowers I only hoped the photographer would come when he had promised. I knew how quickly spiders replace their webs and I certainly didn't want to have to start all over again.

The next day I walked down to the village to meet him and sat on the wooden bench in front of the shop. Everybody collects there in the evening, but now the whole place seemed deserted. It was a beautiful morning. The wedding day storm had cleared the air and we were set fine for September. At last an English car slowed down at the crossroads, we introduced ourselves and rode up to Bel-Air together.

He seemed impressed and soon set to work. He took hundreds of photos of the house, both inside and out and, at the last minute, one of me. When the magazine eventually came out the following September they had chosen some very good shots of the house, but they had also included the one of me. I looked unusually solemn and was, even more unusually, seated at a desk. When I took it down to the farm Grandpa looked at it gravely. 'C'est pas vous,' he said.

'Yes it is,' I insisted. He went to fetch his glasses. He looked closer.

'*Ah oui,*' he conceded. Then he shook his head. '*Mais ... là ... vous êtes trop sévère.*' He screwed up his nose and chuckled.

When *les Fostaires* had visited us the previous year Judith had come from the Parc du Vecors and had told us how beautiful it was. This year they planned to return there briefly *en route* for Italy with Graham and Anne Arnold, both painters. They rang to invite us to join them for four days. We would all be staying in a former monastery in St Croix which was now owned by the *département* and used as a slightly up-market youth hostel. It sounded just what we needed after our hectic summer. Tony and Nan had arrived a few days before with their son and daughter-in-law so, leaving Bel-Air in their capable hands, we set off eastward to cross France, a new experience.

We kept to small roads as far as we were able. I love maps and Tony, a keen fisherman, had brought me a pair of bi-focal fisherman's sunglasses. I no longer had the problem of changing from one pair of spectacles to another, as the amount of magnification for tying flies is perfect for maps. Travelling eastward on roads like corkscrews the landscape varied enormously, as we climbed and then descended the many steep ridges which ran north to south. The rugged countryside had a wild beauty, but the towns were not as flower-decked or as prosperous as those of the south-west, and had an air of dejection. Once we had descended into the Rhône valley the feel of the South returned, and we crossed the river at Loriol and drove on, climbing all the while until we reached St Croix. *Les Fostaires* and Co drove up to the gate, just as we had at last found the monastery.

It was a large rambling building enclosing a central courtyard. Everyone seemed to be having a siesta. We unloaded our bags and, wandering round, eventually found a young man who showed us our rooms, which were at opposite ends of an enormous echoing corridor. It was easy to imagine the monks filing up and down. We had a wonderful view from our window of steep hillsides and a riverbed curving below. It was all so different from our region. This was just what we needed. We caught up with each other's lives, and ate a very good but simple meal of cold meat and salad, seated together on long benches in the courtyard. Our fellow guests turned out to be a team of cyclists. Looking at the surrounding terrain I thought them very brave but *le cyclisme* is a passion all over France.

The nearby town of Die, which we visited briefly after supper, seemed to be a centre of activity. There were several theatre groups performing, a festival of modern music, even a visiting orchestra from Hungary, but we were very tired and, after sharing a bottle of the local, excellent, *Clairette de Die*, we came home. We planned our sightseeing for the following day and said goodnight.

Once in bed, we realised we had chosen the wrong end of the corridor as, from our room, we could hear every footstep from up and down the wide stone stairway. Also the cloakroom and lavatory at the foot of the stairs had a medieval door with an iron latch. As it was lifted it scraped; as it fell it clanged. Both sounds reverberated up the stairs. Ah well, it wouldn't go on all night. We fell asleep.

We were shocked awake by a bright light on our faces. Startled, we sat up. It was only then that we noticed a wide fanlight on the wall above our heads. Anyone using the corridor outside would put on the light and ... we had no choice but to lie listening to a murmured and maddening conversation, too loud to ignore – but not loud enough to understand.

At last the light went out and we fell asleep again, only to be woken some time later by the returning cyclists who, not as tired as we, had clearly stayed much longer in Die and enjoyed many a *verre*. The downstairs latch scraped and clanged repeatedly until, at long last, they all seemed to shuffle off into another part of the monastery and it was quiet. This time it was more difficult to get to sleep but we did ... eventually.

About half an hour later we were dragged once more into desperate and unwilling consciousness. The accursed latch rose and fell and another troop of footsteps came up the echoing stairs. There were voices too – but what language were they speaking? It wasn't French. It wasn't particularly quiet either. But with the next sound I thought I must be so tired I was hallucinating – gypsy violins? Many years before I had learned some Hungarian songs. I was singing in several languages in a small nightclub in the West End, mostly favoured by au pair girls and foreign students. Also on the bill was Ronnie Corbett, at that time relatively unknown. His act then consisted mostly of Noel Coward impressions. They were good but meant absolutely nothing to the audience. 'Mad Dogs and Englishmen' was not what they wanted to hear. He was paid off and I was required to learn yet more songs in Hungarian. Some months later, I included some of these songs in my act at another club, where one of the waiters turned out to be a Hungarian gypsy musician. He invited me to meet his brothers, their wives and their children who all lived together in two rooms in Brixton. While the children sat up in bed, the sheets folded neatly back and secured with large safety pins, the brothers took their instruments from the back of the wardrobe and from under the bed and we made music. This was not the kind of music normally heard in Brixton and people leaned out of their windows to listen. Now in the middle of the night in a monastery – this was the same music.

I began to laugh. My husband did not see the joke, as the haunting tunes went on and on. The Hungarian orchestra were clearly either having a post-mortem on their performance that night in Die or, I suspect, just playing a wind-down after a long tour. Cigarette smoke curled under the door. They were clearly sleeping, or not sleeping in the adjoining rooms. I began to hum the tune. 'For God's sake!' pleaded my exhausted husband. 'It must be nearly dawn.'

At last, once more we slept. Suddenly a horrendous howling forced its way into our unbelieving ears. It was like something in torment. Each time we started to drift off again, it recommenced. The sky was light. We had had almost no sleep. I staggered out of bed. I looked down but could see nothing. It started again. Neighbouring dogs began to bark. It was no use, we might as well get up. Even after a shower we were still reeling from the worst night we had ever had. Not even coping with teething babies could compare and that was a very, very long time ago. We decided that we couldn't possibly stay another night.

We joined the others for breakfast expecting a similar tale but one look at their relaxed and smiling faces told us that at the other end of the vast corridor they had heard absolutely nothing. The girl who served us coffee sympathised. 'Don't worry,' she said. 'Everyone is leaving today. You will have the whole place to yourselves.' The howling it seemed did not often occur. It was just the local dog having a nightmare. Bully for him, I thought, at least he was asleep!

We had no more troubles and the rest of our stay was a delight. We drove up the de Cambeau valley and climbed up to look at the Tête de Praorzel. 1951 metres high, it was spectacular. Judith finds great heights positively intoxicating. She and Barry went as high as they could where they crawled to the edge and looked over, Mike, who loves walking, just set off and disappeared, while Graham and Ann and I sat half-way up, just gazing at the flat-topped head of the mountain, wreathed in fine gossamer cloud. We made a trip south to visit friends who had bought what had been the village post office in Venterol. They were just as much in love with their house as we are with ours, and, also like us, had wonderful French neighbours. We went to market in Nyons; very Provençal with herbs, soap, olive oil, dried flowers and local pottery and, before we left, we bought lavender oil from an old woman in the village of St Croix. Her son harvested the lavender from as high as it would grow. That way the oil is stronger, she told us. I have half a bottle left and one drop in a jug of hot water, can still, after all these years, blow your head off.

Our friends left for Italy and we decided to return to Bel-Air via the Mediterranean. Since having the pool my swimming had improved, and I had a sudden overwhelming longing to swim in the sea. Bernard and Mary Spear, who were to arrive at Bel-Air at the end of the month, had told us many times how beautiful Collioure was. We looked at the map. It couldn't have been much further south without falling into Spain, but off we set. Sadly by the time we got there we were very tired. It was horrendously crowded and, after having tried unsuccessfully to park anywhere, or even to slow down, without getting hooted at, we drove through and never did get to see it. Perhaps one early Spring, or very late summer in the future, we might try Collioure again.

We retreated to Argeles Plage and had two wonderful swims. The sky was blue, the palms waved, the pods on the poinciana trees were full of seeds. Our hotel was small and the Catalan cooking excellent. We were going to stay two nights but we drifted off to sleep to the unwelcome sounds of nearby televisions. At five-thirty in the morning, a metal shutter being thrown up below our window was our first indication of the bakery next door. As they began work on the daily bread, we went down to a deserted beach to swim in the dawn light, came back, showered, had breakfast and left. It was time to go home.

It took us five hours by D roads but we needed the quiet. Bel-Air was waiting for us. Tony and Nan had prepared a meal. We sat together in the blessed peace as the stars came out, and they told us of the previous night down at the farm when they had gently, but firmly, to demur from watching a third video of the wedding.

A few days later I took another look at the decrepit old cupboard which still leaned against the wall in the new room. I knew that English, proprietary brand paint stripper was useless against these old paints.

'Il faut de l'encaustique,' said Claudette. 'Mais – attention! Il faut aussi des gants et des bottes.'

I bought caustic crystals from the *droguerie* and, as she had told me, wearing wellingtons, gloves and even goggles, followed the instructions on the packet. We carried out the cupboard.

'The story of my life,' said Mike to Tony.

'Moving furniture!'

We gingerly turned it flat, and balanced it on top of the workmate. Added to the bucket of water, the caustic bubbled like witches brew. I slopped it all over the surface and, after a few moments, hosed it off. To my amazement the dirt and paint just dissolved and trickled off, and the handsome walnut grain was revealed. It was the most satisfying work. A certain caution was necessary, and I was glad of the goggles, as I later discovered a minute, round burn on the end of my nose. Once the cupboard was dry, we waxed it and repaired it sufficiently to be able to use it as a simple wardrobe. We were very glad that we had not chopped it up.

Before we finally left that summer, it was necessary to make our new, as yet unfinished room, secure. As well as the original window, M. Duparcq had cut the spaces for a new door and a second window. We now needed them filled, and shutters made. We also had to decide what to do with the old window. It had no glass and a very ancient, crude, outside frame and shutter. The small oak beam at the top had warped over the years and looked like an eyebrow, but it was very much a part of Bel-Air.

M. Brut, our original carpenter, who had made our

kitchen cupboards and replaced the old shutters, had retired. M. Parges, a handsome, curly-haired man, was confident that he could do all that was required except the old window. He looked at it doubtfully. Yes – he could quite see that it had a certain charm but – it was extremely old. He wasn't even sure he could make a window to go in that space – mind you if anyone could it would be himself – but – the shutter? He shrugged.

'But you could try?' I pleaded.

'*Bien sur, mais ...* '

Whether it was the fact that he turned out to be Corinne's uncle, or whether he just had second thoughts, he did manage to make a window frame to fit inside. He did repair the shutter, and he did have the grace to say that it looked *très joli* after it was finished. The whole north side of our house, neglected up until this holiday, looked *très jolie*.

I began to plan the new room. We gave the walls a coat of flat white and, as one of the beams came down very low, we asked M. Duparcq if he would add an upright beam at the lower end to stop people walking under it. This he did, but rather crudely and, as the two beams were of different wood, I resolved to paint them the following year and perhaps have a try at stencilling something on them. The weather changed and after our last guests had gone we closed the pool and brought in the furniture. Bernie had entertained us reading Alan Coren aloud and telling us the latest Jewish jokes, but we had needed fires in the evening. The swallows were collecting on the wire. The last sunflowers in the neighbouring fields were dry and almost black, their shrunken heads bent over like rows of rusty nails. It was time to begin packing up. We went to settle our bill with M. Albert, the plumber. He wouldn't take anything for the second-hand washing machine, saying that he had exchanged it for the old gas water heater. I put weedkiller down on my terrace, mulched a few tender plants, and we made a last trip to the *Mammouth* – the hypermarket – to stock up with coffee for the winter, and to buy a few Christmas presents, blackberry liquor and large tins of *confit* – preserved duck. I couldn't imagine any supermarket in England where, at that time, for just over £6 for two, one could eat for lunch, *terrine de sanglier* with a rice and pineapple salad, chocolate flan with pears, and drink a carafe of reasonable red wine. I noticed that *civet de lièvre* was also on the menu, but I doubt it would have been up to Claudette's standard.

We pushed our trolley out under a leaden sky and I knew it was time to return to London. We had always imagined that each year we might want to stay a little longer but, as with all the best laid plans ... we hadn't thought about the difference having a grandchild might make. Now we had one, we found that we missed him. It had been a wonderful summer and there was always the next trip to plan.

13

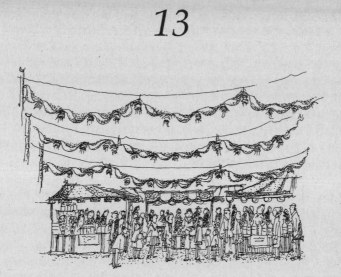

Throughout the winter months in M. Albert's village, anyone with an hour to spare on a Monday evening has but one choice. Our paper flower–making efforts for Véronique's wedding pale into insignificance beside the months of industry in this remote place. Tens of thousands of paper decorations are cut out and put together. They are carefully stored in readiness for the great day, the second Sunday in September, when the whole village will be *en fête* in homage to a simple dried fruit – the prune.

It is impossible to exaggerate the importance of plums to this area. In early spring, the gently rolling hillsides are embroidered with bouquets of white blossom. By the middle of August, the purple fruit hang so heavy on the trees that the branches almost touch the neatly kept ground beneath. For the next few weeks small, crouching armies can be seen beneath the rows. It is backbreaking work for these plums are not picked, but must fall to the ground as each small tree is shaken. When we first came to Bel-Air

Raymond harvested in the traditional way, shinning up a little iron ladder and shaking the branches as hard as he could. Now, like many farmers, he uses a machine. It grasps the slender trunk, unfurls a giant inverted umbrella, shakes the tree and collects the plums which tumble down. But before the machine can start, the ground must be cleared of any which have fallen during the night. And if it rains hard the machine cannot be used at all.

They are special, large plums, *la prune d'Ente*. With a very high sugar content and exceptionally good for drying, they were originally brought back from Damascus during the crusades. The first record of their cultivation in France was in 1148 by monks at the Abbey of Clairac. *Les Pruneaux d'Agen*, as they were soon called, although never actually grown there, became famous throughout France. Cultivated throughout Lot-et-Garonne it was from Agen that they were exported via the *canal du Midi*. Whether going simply to Bordeaux or on to England, the customers reading '*Pruneaux d'Agen*' stamped on the wooden cases soon demanded more under this name.

In 1934 a *Banquet de la Prune* was held in Paris. The glory of this fruit, was celebrated in verses – twenty-seven of them – by a certain M. Gabriel Tallet from Lot-et-Garonne. He clearly feels it necessary to describe other varieties of plum at length, but finishes with:

'*Tous ces fruits sont bons, les nôtres sont mielleurs.*' All these fruit are good, but ours are better.

He then waxes extremely lyrical about his beloved region:

> *L'amour? Il est chez nous le maître. Il nous inspire.*
> *Il est dans le murmure et dans l'appel du vent.*
> *Dans l'arbre qui se penche et la fleur qu'on respire ...*

> And love? For us, it is our master. It inspires us.
> In the murmur of the wind, the leaning tree, the perfume of our flowers.

There were many in Paris that night who were originally from the south-west. After all twenty-seven verses, I doubt there was a dry eye in the house.

M. Albert's village of St Aubin is surrounded by plum orchards and in 1985 they decided to revive an ancient tradition. *La Foire aux Pruneaux* was reborn. It was a great success and each year becomes ever more splendid, attracting thousands of visitors. All the organisation is done by the local inhabitants. Cars must be left in selected fields on the outskirts and each entrance to the village is bright with welcoming banners of paper flowers stretching across the road. Once the small entrance fee is paid, hands are marked with a rubber stamp, and you may come and go as you please throughout the day. It is a scene of great jollity. The garlands of thousands of paper flowers which have been so painstakingly made are strung closely across the streets to make continuous tunnels of colour. There are about a hundred stalls which, as well as selling local specialities, display every conceivable use for *les Pruneaux*.

There are prunes in cakes, tarts and ice-cream. Prunes made into jam, prunes covered in chocolate, prunes stoned and stuffed with almond paste, prunes preserved in Armagnac or *Eau de Vie*, and, most spectacular of all, prunes used to replace apples in the local special pie called a *tourtière*.

This is made with layer upon layer of a local version of strudel pastry which is very carefully pulled out by hand until it covers the whole length of a farm table. After being left to dry until transparent, it is cut into rough circles. The first three cover the bottom of a round and buttered tin. The next are layered with sugar, fruit and alcohol. The last few scraps of pastry are twisted into curls and piled as high as possible like a fantastic wig. It is absolutely delicious when fresh but very difficult to make. It is a skill that is handed down. Both Grandma and Claudette are experts but I've tried and failed miserably. One of the highlights of the *Foire au Pruneaux* is a demonstration by a local expert and people jostle for position to watch every detail.

The stall holders dress in the traditional costume of long skirts, lace collars and caps or, for the men, narrow black ties and a beret. The local band from Monflanquin, in white trousers, scarlet shirts and black capes and berets parade past the stalls. They have a mixed repertoire but I think the young ones prefer 'When the saints go marching in'.

At nine-thirty in the morning the stands are judged. There will be prizes both for the best display of prunes and the best costumes. At ten o'clock Mass is celebrated by the Bishop of Agen. He is greatly loved because he is a local man and speaks Occitan, the patois which the old people still use to one another. Sometimes he takes a special Mass completely in Occitan. His sermons are directed to those who work the land. He understands and encourages them and they hang on his every word. After the Mass he processes to the centre of the village where the garlands stretch in a giant spider's web between the church and the Mairie. Surrounded by a huge crowd, he blesses first the tray of the most beautiful prunes and then the two small, costumed girls who carry it. Laying his hands on the children's heads, he gives a blessing for all harvests and those who gather them. He talks of the duty to share all the fruits of the earth. A choir of old people sing lustily in Occitan, finishing with '*Se canto che canté*', a very old song of parted lovers, the bishop joining in as loudly as anyone else.

The aperitif, a cocktail of '*eau de vie de prune*' topped up with sparkling white wine, and with a prune in the bottom of the glass, sustains the good humour. There is no shortage of things to eat. Skewers of hot prunes wrapped in bacon taste especially good and help to sustain one through the somewhat lengthy inauguration speeches by everyone who is anyone in the local hierarchy. At 12.30 the midday meal is served. This year the menu was: *Pâté en croûte, pintade flambée* (guinea fowl), *petits légumes de saison, salade, fromage,*

128

mousse de pruneaux. And all for 75 Francs with *'vin compris'*.

In the afternoon they have the judging of the best song about *'les Pruneaux'* in French or in Occitan, or the best painting. One year there was a race to see who could fastest arrange a large basket of raw plums into a flat tray ready for the oven. The trays in which the plums are slowly dried into prunes are called *claies*. As the ovens have developed they have changed their shape. At first plums were simply left in the sun to dry. Then, perhaps after a few wet summers, they began to use the family oven. Next, as more plums were grown, came the circular ovens, especially built with very small bricks. For this oven, or *étuve*, the trays made in the winter from willow, were shaped like the petals of a flower. The whole circle had to be turned to ensure the even drying of the fruit. The oven on Raymond's farm, still in occasional use, was the next development. Larger and taller, it enables more plums to be dried at a time. An iron trolley with a dozen or more shelves is loaded with the flat trays of plums. It is then pushed along a metal track into the oven which is heated by a wood fire in a pit outside, the heat being conveyed by thick metal pipes which line the walls. When we first bought Bel-Air we too had an *étuve*. The high narrow doors still have the slot where the thermometer rested. At that time it was home to a family of hedgehogs who shuffled in and out at night. It had not been used for plums for many years and had an old copper built into the end wall for cooking the pig. Having neither plums nor pig, we cleared it out and, eventually, put in a window and made it into a pleasant, small studio.

At the *Foire aux Pruneaux* the revelry continues until the evening with donkey rides for the children and various entertainments on a rough stage. There is usually a visiting folk dance group leaping about with enthusiasm, often with traditional instruments.The dancers often have a great age-range, grandparents passing down the skills to quite small children.

There is a travelling still, called an *alambic*, with which a large and bucolic gentleman demonstrates exactly how the lethal *Eau de Vie de Prune* is officially distilled. You may buy a litre for 100 francs.

At seven o'clock in the evening, just in case anyone is still hungry, long tables are laid in an open-ended barn. For fifty francs you can enjoy a great helping of a *daube* of beef with – naturally – prunes, followed by cheese and a *pâtisserie* and as much wine as you can drink. There is dancing as long as there is anyone left to dance but, at the crack of dawn, the more energetic young men and women are already busy taking down the decorations. The *Foire aux Pruneaux* is over for another year.

In February, while the villagers of St Aubin were busy making garlands, Philippe, the Bertrand's son, was with us in London, struggling with a course in commercial English. It was paid for by the sugar company for which he works. He would come home exhausted every night, still with hours of homework to complete. His English has always been quite good although he has few opportunities to practise it, but this was a new language both to him and to us, full of business jargon, and I'm afraid we weren't much help to him. It was interesting to contrast this serious young man, missing his wife and baby son, with the carefree young teenager who had first come to stay with us so many years before. I think that by the end of the fortnight he couldn't wait to get back to France and by the middle of April, neither could we.

London was cold and grey but Bel-Air was like another world. The sunlight was brilliant and everything was leafing so fast you could almost see it happening. The meadow was lush with buttercups and yellow trefoil, honesty flowered around the well. Leaves on the ash and the fig trees were uncurling, the reprieved roses were all in bud and the wisteria already had a tinge of lavender.

Anaïs's white irises under the window were especially beautiful this spring and unobscured by burgeoning thistles – the last minute weedkiller on the terrace had worked a treat. Only the miner bees were scurrying about, forever tidying up their neat cylindrical holes. Five bits of mallow that I had just pushed into the soft ground the day before leaving in September had all rooted. The syringa was in bud. The flowers on the *viburnum opulus*, in their disguise of pale green to match the leaves, were waiting to gradually change to the spectacular white which gives them their common name *boule de neige.*

There was such a charge of energy in the air, and a house and garden which are completely neglected for seven months can really make use of it. We had a call from Jack and Bess, our friends from Scotland. They were thinking of coming. Would it be all right? This was to be very much a working holiday but as they were the sort of people who change houses every few years in order to start renovations all over again, we had no qualms about their arrival.

One of the tasks we had decided to tackle this holiday was the outside woodwork. We had at one time considered painting our shutters the very pale grey which is traditional in the villages. But having done one, it looked wrong. Most of the old shutters one sees have not been repainted for many years, and it is this very bleached powdery look which is so attractive. The new paint was much less so.

Now we had three pairs of shutters on the new room which M. Parges had treated with a very sympathetic product which, as well as preserving the wood, gave it a rich, slightly oily look. We decided to sand off what remained of our old woodstain and re-do all the remaining shutters. While we were at the *Bricomart*, the local DIY store, we saw some very attractive, large, off-white floor tiles. They were on promotion at 68 francs a square metre. We knew they would be perfect for the new room in the *chai*, making it much lighter. We rushed home to measure up and were extremely lucky as twenty-one square metres was all they had left. We had done all the previous tiling of the bedroom floors ourselves but we felt we were past tackling this one. Once you have tiled three floors there's not much of a challenge left – or so we told ourselves. In any case we were too busy in the garden, building a rockery, devising a way of moving heavy stones as though bulldozers had never been invented, and dividing clumps of perennials.

The cows had come up for the summer but were still in the lower field so we were able to shovel barrow-loads of last year's dried manure from the hard stand on the other side of the barn. We spread as much as we could. We have found that leaving it in a pile is hopeless. It is impossible to find in the summer under its waist-high cover of flourishing weeds.

The seeds which I had collected from the previous year's morning glories and planted on our arrival had already germinated. Before we left we sowed nasturtiums, and cosmos, yet more morning glories and *cobea scandens* – a plant I have never succeeded in growing – and we just hoped it would rain before too long.

Raymond, a piece of the first lilac of spring tied to his tractor, came up to inspect the wheat which patterned *le grand champ* with stripes of brilliant green.

'You'll miss the sunflowers this year,' he said.

It was true. Unfortunately they can only be planted every three years as they take so much out of the soil. By the time we arrived in the summer the wheat would be harvested and the straw made into those great round bales which make such wonderful shapes as the sunlight sinks lower across the wide field.

Before we left we called M. Duparcq. He came up in his old van, pronounced the tiles *chouette* – great – and promised to have the floor finished before we came back in July, and also to tidy and point the outside wall where the door and the window had been cut. I went down to the farm to give Biggles's cage a last-minute clean. We hadn't moved him up to his summer quarters as the nights were chilly. Véronique was in the kitchen having a lesson in making a *tourtière*. Claudette was giving her usual brisk advice. Grandma said very little but I could see she was both pleased and proud that the ancient skill was not to be lost. I watched Véronique. She had a dignity about her and was clearly happy. Jean-Michel, who seemed to have had a variety of jobs before he was married, was now helping Raymond and attending agricultural college one day a week. No one said anything but clearly the new son-in-law was going to be the answer to a great many problems. How very clever of Véronique to have chosen him.

It is always hard to leave when the weather in spring is as wonderful as it was that year. We went for a last drive and came home by yet another small and winding road that was new to us. As we turned a corner we stopped in amazement. All along the edge of a wood, on the bank, in the ditch and on into the wood itself were row upon row of a tall elegant plant that I had never seen before. The flowers, on long slender stems, were white above shiny pointed leaves. They looked like bleached red-hot pokers. There were hundreds as far as the eye could see and yet, at the edge of the wood they stopped, and in the next copse there were none. I ran back to pick a few and took them to Claudette. She had no idea what they were and I had to wait till I got back to London to find that I had seen a wood full of rare asphodels.

Early summer in London was unexpectedly hot. All my thin, cool dresses were, of course, in France. I spent a great deal of time in the Theatre Museum in Covent Garden doing research for a play I was writing. Although the staff are unfailingly helpful it was no weather to be working indoors, let alone underground.

We finally packed up and left for France and on the way

down made a detour once more into George Sand country. This time, not to the Château of Nohant, but some thirty miles east to the village of Gargilesse. George Sand, at the age of forty-six, fell deeply in love with a young friend of her son, Maurice. Alexandre Manceau was an engraver who exhibited regularly in Paris. Maurice had first met him at the studio of Delacroix and invited him to spend time at Nohant. Intending to stay for several weeks in fact he remained there for fifteen years. He had the same fervour for work as she but always put her first. He was neat, graceful and above all, totally devoted to her.

As her literary and political fame grew so did the crowds of admirers to Nohant. Even when in Paris, she was constantly besieged by devotees. Elizabeth and Robert Browning were among those who asked to meet her. Eventually Manceau saw the need for a bolt-hole for them both.

In June 1857 they went on a trip to the valley of the river Creuse. The countryside was remote and wild, like a miniature Switzerland. They came to the village of Gargilesse and found there not only a micro-climate with rare butterflies, but a simple, hard-working community and, best of all, a small cottage for sale, tucked away down a winding lane. Manceau bought it for her – a rare treat for George Sand who worked all her life to provide for a great many dependents – and he decorated and equipped it. There she wrote in perfect peace, completing thirteen novels, as well as many essays and several plays.

'The weather is wonderful, hot and bright,' she wrote. 'Manceau has gone catching butterflies. I've stayed here to finish my novel. 620 pages in 24 days! I have never worked with such pleasure as at Gargilesse.'

Sadly their happiness together was not to last. Although much younger than her, he died of consumption. Only too familiar with the symptoms of this scourge of the nineteenth century from which Chopin had also eventually died, she nursed Manceau devotedly until the end.

Gargilesse is still remote, even today. That morning it had been raining since breakfast but as we got nearer the sun appeared. The village is very sheltered and ferns and stonecrop grow out of the old garden walls. We asked the way at the shop.

'Just up the street, you can't miss it ... '

A young student sat reading a book as we entered and, apart from her, we had the place to ourselves. It is very small and left very much as it used to be. I gently touched George Sand's little button boots which lay on the simple bed, and thought about the girl who wore her first boots with such relief and delight so long ago, as she bounded along the Paris pavements.

14

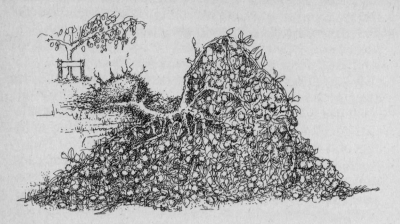

We drove on through the luxuriant lanes, finding a place for a picnic by a small stream. It was getting hotter and the strong sun was dazzling through the trees. Anxious to avoid Limoges we took an unfamiliar route. We were on our way to St Junien when we saw the first sign. We said nothing. A few miles further on there was another. This time it would be only a five-minute detour. We looked at each other. We simply couldn't just drive by. Much has been written about Oradour sur Glane. To see it for myself was an experience I do not regret.

The surrounding countryside is so beautiful. The small road winds through green banks lush with cow parsley. It is impossible to imagine that one of the most grim sights in all France is forever preserved around the next corner. What must it be like to live in the new Oradour built outside? The people there were shopping, going about their daily lives as we drove through and followed the sign *'Village des Martyrs'*.

The village is enclosed. There were few visitors. The signs asking for quiet are hardly necessary. To walk those blackened, desolate streets is chilling. Each place is marked where groups of men from the village were shot by the SS and then burned in heaps. No birds sing. Nothing grows. I don't know whether they deliberately kill any vegetation which might have, in time, softened this desecration.

It was General De Gaulle, taken to the village a few days after D-day in 1944, who commanded that a wall be built around this village and that it be left as a memorial and a witness. More than fifty years on, witnesses are harder to find and doubly important.

We walked slowly up to the church and on entering found a small group with a guide. We listened. He was a sweet-faced man with prematurely grey hair. His parents had lived in Oradour. He owed his very existence, he told us, to the fact that on that day – 10 June 1944 – a wedding had been held in a nearby town, and his young parents, not then married, had been invited. He described very quietly the horrors of that day and the very matter-of-factness of it all. He told of the man cutting hay on the edge of the village, the young German looking at his map, checking the boundary as if doing a survey, and then telling him to go away as he was on the right side of the line.

Among those on the wrong side that day were the 247 children in the school. Only one of them survived. An evacuee from Lorraine, he had already experienced the brutality of the Germans and when, at two o'clock in the afternoon, lorries full of SS men in battledress arrived and everyone was told to assemble on the big village green, he ran away.

No one else suspected anything. They were used to seeing the odd German vehicle pass through the village but that was all. There had never been any trouble. Someone said it was just an identity card check. A group of six cyclists rode into the village. They, unfortunately, had crossed to the wrong side of the line.

When the men were separated from the women and children, fears began to grow. From the church where they were imprisoned, frantic women heard the sound of gunfire and must have smelled the smoke. In the village, as the bodies of the men were piled and burned, a few escaped by feigning death and later crawling out. But the church was not to be a sanctuary for the 500 women and children locked inside. The Germans first filled it with suffocating smoke. In the panic and chaos, one woman managed to climb out of a window and eventually survived, although she was badly injured in the hail of gunfire with which the SS then massacred every other woman and child. Last of all they set fire to the church.

'Imagine the anguish of people in nearby hamlets who had, that morning, sent their children to school, as they saw the smoke rising from Oradour,' said the guide. 'There was nothing they could do. They could not get near. The whole place was sealed off. And later, almost worst of all, a concertina and sounds of revelry could be heard across the fields. The SS men sang as they looted the houses. It was not until the early hours of the morning that the troops moved out of Oradour, leaving everything burning behind them.'

'But – why did they do it?' asked a small woman, in tears as we all were.

The guide shook his head. 'No one really knows – perhaps simply to frighten the French people and stop them collaborating with the Allies after the D-day landings.'

'I'm from Canada,' said a man at the edge of the group. 'I just want to ask –' He paused. 'Do you ever have German tourists here?'

'Oh yes,' said the guide. 'And – they tell me they are very fearful. They see the same spirit amongst a few of their young, and –' he added firmly, 'I have had my whole life to think about this and I tell you – they were very young. The ones who did this. They were at that stage in life, you understand, when they were emancipated from their families, but, as yet, had no commitment, no wives, no children. This is the dangerous time, Monsieur, when anyone can be corrupted by false ideals. It can happen in any country.'

'Animals!' sobbed one of the listeners.

'*Pire!*' answered the guide. Worse!

We returned slowly to the gate. As we drove back into the present we were glad we had turned off our route. As a very young soldier my husband was among the troops who liberated Belsen concentration camp. We were married for almost twenty years before he told me, or could talk about, what he saw.

It was early evening by the time we reached Bel-Air. The sun was still shining. Raymond declared that we must have brought it with us as, unlike England, they had had a disastrous June. 'The hay crop was all but ruined,' he said. 'But your garden looks pretty,' he added.

It was the morning glories that must have caught his eye. Although that day's blooms were closing, the plants were everywhere, trailing up their poles where I had planted the new seeds and where I had simply scattered pods from the previous year, trailing everywhere else they could find a space. We had two weeks in which to get the house and garden into some sort of order to welcome our first guests. We brought Biggles up to his summer quarters outside the front door. One morning, thinking he might like a change of scene, I foolishly put him on the ground under the ash tree. Ten minutes later there was a mad flurry of wings as a kestrel swooped on the cage and did its best to get him out. Biggles looked petrified. I thought he might die of fright, but once back in the safety of the porch he chirped away as though nothing had happened.

We had a succession of guests that summer, many of

whom had never been before, but they all seemed to fit in. We also christened the campsite. Behind the slope down from the wall where the laurels shelter the pool, we have a wide strip of grass. As it is our only level piece of ground we thought it might be good for anyone with a tent, and so it has subsequently proved. But our first campers arrived from Switzerland in a smart, two-storey camping van. Geneviève, one of my first au pairs with whom I have always kept in touch, came with her son, a friend and two more children.

Seven-year-old Alexandru leaned out of the top bunk. 'Good morning!' he shouted. His mother laughed; it was nearly dusk. 'It's his only English word,' she said. 'He was determined to use it.'

They stayed a few days and then went south as our next guests reached Bel-Air. It seemed extremely quiet without the children as Ivor sat drawing the bales of straw in the great field with increasing boldness and Marian kindly read the script of my play and gave me lots of good advice. While they worked by the pool, Mike and I were busy finishing the new bedroom with its striking floor of white tiles. We treated all the woodwork with an anti-woodworm product and gave the walls another coat of flat white. The worst job was sanding a crude overhead beam which, unlike the massive oak beams, was a later addition. I had bought a copy of Jocasta Innes's *Paint Magic* and I was full of enthusiasm but it didn't make the sander any lighter or my arm ache less.

Eventually the beam was smooth enough to undercoat. Then came the real fun. We mixed a very pale green for the beam and the upright that joined it. Would it work? It did. We gave it another coat; so far so good. We had brought stencil paper from London and Mike cut a simple stencil of a curving stem and five leaves. We mixed a slightly darker green, and beginning at the highest point we twined the stencilled design round the beam. Once so ugly, the beam was transformed and we began to realise just how compulsive stencilling can be. We looked at the wall where the bed would go. With another stencil with a straight stem we began at the door and, as though the garden was creeping in, we brought the stems and leaves up from the floor for about two feet and continued round as far as the bed. Then we stopped, which was not easy. Without Mike's restraining hand I might well have turned the whole room into a leafy jungle.

We went off to buy a bed and came home with it on top of the car. Just as I was laundering sheets for the next guests, the second-hand washing machine which M. Albert had installed the previous summer began to shudder and refused to spin. As phonecalls produced no immediate response, it was like a miracle when we had a totally unexpected call from our friend, Louis of all trades, in London. He and Helen were on their way to the Olympics in Barcelona and begging a bed for the following night. Did he have his tools with him? Yes. Wonderful! It was just as well, for we had five French guests for the next two nights and friends from Germany were due any moment. It was a full house. Raymond and Claudette came up almost every night to swim and afterwards there would be long discussions round the pool. When guests enjoy themselves together it is a great pleasure to sit back and watch them. Apart from clean sheets, they all know that there is no service at Bel-Air.

The new room was finished just in time for what was becoming my cousin David's annual visit. For the first time he was bringing with him his partner Charles. David gave up his parish in Notting Dale to found the charity CARA – Care and Resources for Aids. Having always refused to make any compromises about his own homosexuality – not easy as a priest – he felt passionately that the church was failing to address the whole problem of Aids. CARA was his answer. I had never sat on a committee in my life but he persuaded me to become a trustee. David is very good at talking people into extending their talents, and working for CARA has certainly changed my life.

Sadly Charles was already very sick and this was, for him, a kind of farewell tour. They had started in Amsterdam where they both spoke at the fourth World Aids Conference, then went on to Germany to visit Charles's sister before dropping down to Cluny to go to Taizé. This is a religious community, founded by a monk directly after the war, to promote religious tolerance. It has become a meeting place for many thousands of young people of every religion, and Charles had always wanted to see it. Their next stop was to be with us. I have worked in the theatre for many years and people's sexual orientation has never been a problem for me, but I did wonder how Raymond and Claudette would react. They knew and loved David, but Charles was a beautiful Greek Cypriot, and with his long hair and unashamedly camp manner – *on verra*.

As usual, it is not the things that one worries about that come to pass. Charles could charm the birds from the trees. He had a totally disarming frankness. During the day David would take him to all his favourite places and at night we would sit under the stars and talk in a way that I don't think would have been possible with anyone else.

One night there was a sudden storm. It didn't last long but there were a few minutes of a tornado-like wind and the next morning we were horrified to see that five, heavily laden plum trees in the orchard near us had blown down. Mike went to fetch Hugh and all morning they worked with Raymond and Jean-Michel to winch the trees up and then lash them to a strong bar set between two posts. It wasn't long before Grandpa came up. He looked on suspiciously.

'*C'est les racines*,' he said to me quietly. 'The roots have loosened. Shaking them about with that machine. I told them but ...' he shrugged. I thought he just might have a point but I said nothing.

On Sunday we all went out to lunch at La Petite Auberge at Villefranche. It was, as usual, very good. While we were sleeping it off by the pool we opened one eye to see David and Charles driving off quietly down the track.

'Where on earth are they going now?' asked Mike and fell asleep again.

That evening, as we sat idly under the porch, our friends the Thomases arrived looking very elegant and bearing champagne. We had hardly recovered when Hugh and Sally and their children appeared with gifts, closely followed by Raymond and Claudette and the two old people. David and Charles carried out an enormous cake and everyone wished us a happy wedding anniversary. How David knew is a mystery. We are so bad at anniversaries that, when we bought Bel-Air and could not remember the exact date of our marriage, the *notaire* did not believe that we were married at all. It was pure pleasure to have a fête arranged by somebody else. We sang and drank many toasts and it was an evening I shall never forget.

All through August, family and friends came and went, each bringing their own interests. Some wrote, some painted and others simply ate, slept and swam and recharged their batteries. The weather was perfect. We bought a summer cover for the pool. Made of bubble plastic, it floated on the surface of the water and retained the heat during the night. It also prevented leaves and dust blowing in and hence reduced the amount of cleaning.

We hoped that the cover would enable us to swim right up to the beginning of October but once the new September moon arrived it brought the rain with it. Every few days we would have yet another heavy downpour and we began to worry about the increasing amount of leaks in our roof. The problem was not the roof itself; the tiles were sound, but the underlying rafters, and more especially the *voliges* – the ancient laths which crossed them, and supported the tiles – were beginning to sag. This caused hollows in which the water collected and, eventually, it found its way through. The ping of drips into buckets began to haunt us.

When we had first set eyes on Bel-Air the tumbling roof tiles had been part of the charm of the place, at least to me, even the great hole through which one could see the sky while standing in the living room. But once we had bought the house, renewing the roof was our first priority and we thought it had been adequately done. We had indeed asked the *charpentier* to replace all the wood that was necessary, but he had clearly only changed the bare minimum. Also when he had retiled he had used new, flat 'stop' tiles which lock into place underneath the ancient curved top tiles. They prevent the upper tiles from sliding down, especially useful when the Mirages from the French Airforce occasionally splinter out of the distance to shatter the countryside with sonic booms. *La tuile stop* is a sensible idea but it makes the roof heavier and gradually bends the *voliges*.

'We've got another leak,' said Mike gloomily one lunchtime after we had been helping with the plums.

Raymond was sympathetic. 'You can never make these roofs completely watertight,' he said. 'But perhaps you should ask M. Lecours to take a look. Before the pigeon season,' he added with a grin.

A few days later M. Lecours joined us in the attic. It runs the length of the house, and at the far end, a doorway has been cut through the thick wall into the later addition. After you crouch to pass through, if you turn back you can clearly see how the newest section of the house was just added on, against the chimney wall, as a child might build with toy bricks. There is a border of white in the crepis and a broad splash of blue where, on this once-outside, end wall of the house a vine was long ago treated with copper sulphate. How long ago I still do not know. Madame Esther thinks that it was her grandfather who enlarged the house, and he was born at Bel-Air in 1839. I believe that at one time the family slept up in the attic while the animals were stabled below. As I often do, I stood in the attic trying to imagine the three little boys sleeping on their narrow straw palliasses.

M. Lecours was in more practical mood. He confirmed our fears. The rafters were in reasonable shape – perhaps it might be prudent to replace one or two. The problem was the waney-edged laths which went across between them at about twelve inch intervals. These, he advised, needed completely replacing with a solid boarding. 'There's no urgency,' he said, thinking no doubt of the fast approaching pigeon season. 'I could do it for you in the spring.'

He gave us a price which made us wince, but we knew his charges were always the most reasonable. In any case we realised that it was sixteen years since we had first had the roof done. Mike announced that his days of climbing up to fix slipping tiles were definitely over and we ordered the work for the following April.

It was about this time that Dan arrived.

'I'm getting this young man to help with the plums,' said Raymond one evening as he sat drinking a pastis under the porch. He looked slightly worried. 'He's been staying with someone who works with bees and produces honey but now they've arranged for him to come to me. He said he works all right but ...' He shook his head. 'I don't know how I'm going to understand Romanian.'

'Romanian?'

'Yes. It's some scheme or other. For farmers ...' Raymond was vague.

'How long is he coming for?'

'A month!'

'But ... surely that's good!'

Raymond has plenty of help when the children are on holiday but once they go back to school he has a problem with the plum harvest. This seemed to us to be the answer.

'Perhaps he'll have some French,' we encouraged.

The next evening after supper Raymond and Claudette came up to Bel-Air bringing with them a slight, pale, dark-haired young man with a drooping moustache and large soulful eyes. He was polite and grave and, in fact, spoke good French.

'Are you going to be a farmer?' I asked.

He shook his head and looked at me coolly.

'No,' he said. 'When I have finished my studies I shall hope to be a diplomat.'

Raymond looked even more worried.

We saw a great deal of Dan over the next few weeks and watched him change. At first intensely suspicious, he told us that he considered democracy a system with little or no virtue. Elitism was his ideology and he was clearly puzzled by the relationship between Mike and me and Raymond and Claudette. As far as he was concerned there was little a university lecturer, even a retired one, could have in common with a simple farmer. He worked conscientiously enough but he was always uneasy, almost disapproving. When Raymond and Claudette came up to swim he would sit by the pool, lost in some dream or other. He rarely swam. Claudette tried in vain to fatten him up. He often asked us the price of various things in England such as televisions and cameras, and seemed reluctant to believe us. This young Romanian was a curious mixture of sophistication and naïvety.

But during his stay he had a birthday. We were surprised to learn that he was only twenty-three; he looked much older, the effect of the moustache no doubt. As always Claudette made much of the occasion. She bought a special tart, we drank champagne, sang *bon anniversaire* and gave him gifts and suddenly the intending diplomat became a homesick young man. His suspicion finally faded and in his last few days he really seemed to enjoy himself. He gave us a plate before he left which he had brought from home and a woven bag. He wrote to us several times but we have heard nothing now for several years. He sent Raymond a photograph of his wedding. We wonder sometimes how Dan the diplomat is faring and what influence, if any, that summer had.

The heavy, early morning dews of September turned the little tamarisk we had planted on the edge of the now uninhabited camp into a bouquet from some frosty legend by Hans Christian Andersen. In the morning sunlight hundreds of webs glittered, straddling the tops of the tall grasses, a ripple of silver in the breeze. Against the wall of the *chai* the morning glories were still managing a few last blooms and the *cobea scandens* had three buds. Would they open before we had to leave? The virginia creeper was already vivid with red leaves and purple berries on scarlet stems.

   The village below shone in the sunlight but the valley of the Lot and the hills beyond it were shrouded in a rolling mist which the sun would slowly burn away. On the other side of the house there was one more field to harvest. Raymond had enlarged it a few years previously by clearing some of the trees at the edge of the wood. One year he had planted sunflowers. This year, due to the abundant rain, there was a magnificent crop of maize. He talked one morning of planting vines there. This was the first we had heard of it. A new vineyard sloping down towards the house was an attractive proposition.

The maize harvested, today the wood is full of *cèpe* seekers. This highly prized edible fungus – *boletus edulis* – has just began to thrust upward from its moist, subterranean hideout and the hunt is on. They are already selling in the market for over 100F a kilo. These are free – if you can find them – and if you have the right to pick them. The cars of

147

family or friends go slowly up the track to the wood, rest an hour or two and return. We greet the patient gatherers.

'Did you get any?'

'Oh ... not many.' They are cagey. We peer into the bag, the better to identify them ourselves – if we can be bothered to go searching. They usually have less than a kilo, many of them nibbled by passing creatures in this world of the wood where everything eats everything else. Later Claudette appears silently, stick in hand, wearing her apron and wellington boots. She sits down under the porch and proudly shows her kilos of beautiful specimens.

'I thought you were tired yesterday,' I say, making her a tisane.

'Oh ça,' she shrugs. '*Aujourd'hui c'est différent. Chercher des champignons*' – she grins, '*c'est un vice!*'

Our last visitors arrived, my friend Bridget and her old friend Marianne. No stranger to Bel-Air, Marianne, indomitable at eighty-two, insisted on working in the garden and was only slightly miffed when stung by a wasp. Baring her ample buttock she came in and asked calmly for a dab of vinegar.

A neighbour had offered me a white buddleia and I had been waiting for the right moment to transplant it. 'Now!' said Marianne firmly and off we went to get it. Marianne was enchanted with the neighbour's house and garden and took many photographs. We were less enchanted with the buddleia bush which, although magnificent, was about three times as large as we had anticipated. We stuffed it as best we could into the back of the car and drove home. Marianne took charge of both the planting and the pruning and it still survives.

Intensely curious about everything she was such an appreciative guest and gave me a wonderful lesson in how to grow old, not exactly gracefully – that wasn't her style – but certainly gratefully. When I offered to make her a sandwich for the return journey she declined, informing me that she never travelled anywhere without a knife and a very small block of three-ply. Bridget later told me that she also carried a handkerchief square of gingham and a fish-paste jar in which to put a flower – if only a dandelion – to decorate a picnic.

The weather deteriorated. Every day it rained. We were inundated with small, bright green tree frogs. Claudette explained that normally they would stay close to the pond for moisture but as this autumn was fast becoming the wettest on record they roamed at will. They straddled the glazing bars of the windows and our eye would be distracted by their pale underbellies and manic legs as they suddenly changed positions, holding on with the suction pads underneath their tiny feet. Their extraordinarily loud croak would surprise us from the most unexpected places. One, especially intrepid, would balance on the neck of an old wine bottle on the porch, his serenade like a ship lost in the fog.

There were also dozens of snails which would peram-bulate after every shower. Not wanting everything in the garden eaten, I started collecting them to take down to the farm where Philippe stores them in a special cage. There they are fed on flour or dry pasta for one or two weeks to clean them before they are cooked. Claudette always grumbles at this task for *escargots* are one of the few dishes she does not like. I must admit I agree with her but both Raymond and Philippe adore them.

After all that rain the paths around the house became slippery with a kind of land seaweed. I had always been intrigued with this primitive but highly efficient form of life which I had never seen anywhere else, and I was fascinated by the way it almost vanished in hot dry weather. It amused visiting children when I would tell them to pick up what looked like a minute scrap of black paper in amongst the gravel on the path and left for an hour in a saucer of water, it would miraculously turn into a fat greenish lump of seaweed. In a day it would treble in size like some science fiction monster but I had no idea what it was until one year I took some back to England.

Dr Gill Douglas, a botanist at the Natural History Museum, identified it for me, even sending me a couple of photographs at 500x magnification. It was a blue-green alga called *Nostoc Commune*. As she told me that it is especially common in Alpine meadows, Arctic tundra and golf courses I am still at a loss to understand why it has been bordering my path at Bel-Air for as long as I can remember. In the Orient it is apparently cultivated. Some species are used as a valuable fertiliser as it is capable of fixing atmospheric nitrogen. She told me that it is also edible. But I'm not sure that Raymond would be keen to try *'omelette au nostoc'!*

One evening after supper before we left, Véronique was bouncing Philippe's little son Clément on her knee. She looked sideways at Jean-Michel and then announced that Clément would be getting a little cousin the following spring. No-one said anything. I rose to give her a hug, feeling that some sort of congratulation was in order and then everyone followed suit. Jean-Michel looked relieved.

'I was afraid you were going to say "Well – you might have waited a bit longer,"' he said.

As well as constant rain now it began to get colder. This was the spur we needed to order the installation of power points. We had begun to use a word processor in London and knew that, as far as our writing was concerned, there was no turning back to the tedium of a typewriter. We called on M. Fernandez in Monflanquin, described what we wanted, and were promised that the work would be completed before we returned in the spring. We chopped wood and made great roaring fires, but it was very cold getting up in the mornings. Bel-Air is, as far as we are concerned, a house for the summer. If we were going to live there year round we would have to make many radical changes which would inevitably alter the whole character of the house. When the weather gets as bad as this, we leave. It was tedious trying to pack up while at the same time having to dry sodden clothes around the fires but it was, it seemed, raining all over France. The first *cobea* finally opened and I picked it and took it down to Grandma. She was very intrigued as she had never seen such a flower before.

We decided to make the long journey home less irksome by treating ourselves to a night of luxury at the Hotel du Lion d'Or at Romorantin. Friends had told us of the old-fashioned comfort and the wonderful cuisine. What we hadn't realised was that it had since upgraded itself to a *Relais et Chateaux*. We booked a room, closed the house and set off the following day.

After two weeks of chilly discomfort in overalls and mudcaked wellingtons the contrast was almost dreamlike. Emerging from a long soak in a sumptuous bathroom to lie on an exquisite bed and punch up the evening's menu on the television before descending for an aperitif was just what we needed. We began to realise that the Lion d'Or had gone seriously upmarket but we didn't care. Downstairs, after bringing us our drinks, the immaculate, black-coated waitress bowed low and spread a napkin on our laps for the eating of a minute wafer of beef fillet in a sauce with shreds of mint. A tiny vol-au-vent filled with *Trompette de la Mort* – a highly prized black champignon – was followed by a curl of smoked salmon.

The dining room, in pale blues and greens, was not large but calm and hushed. Waiters stood unobtrusively but missed nothing. When Mike accidentally touched his glass with his butter knife it was quietly replaced. I started with a risotto of wild rice with langoustines, flavoured with cardamom. Mike also had langoustines *'rôties à la poudre fine d'épices douces'* which turned out to be cumin. Next I ordered turbot with deep fried shredded vegetables in celery salt, while Mike chose noisettes of lamb *'au tabac de cuisine'* which on enquiry was powdered wild mushroom. They were both absolutely wonderful. The cheese board covered the top of not one but two trolleys. We didn't really need cheese but we had been drinking a Gerwürtstraminer with the fish and hadn't quite finished the good Bordeaux.

I had been told that the puddings at the Lion d'Or were fabulous and that there was the opportunity to have half portions in order to sample more. I am a pig for puddings but only if they are not too sweet. These were perfect. We shared a pancake filled with crushed raspberries, a spicy, dark chocolate ice-cream and a souffle of peaches cooked with redcurrants. I'm sure if I had the money to eat like that every night I would probably long for bangers and mash but it was a memorable meal.

I wrote it all down to send it in my next letter to Claudette and wished she could have shared it with us. We relived it all for the rest of the rain soaked journey home. We knew that when the Barclaycard bill came in, our night out was going to be expensive. What we could not have envisaged was its arrival on Black Wednesday. For us the pound had fallen at the worst possible moment and until, or if ever, it improved, it would certainly have to be a once in a lifetime experience!

15

The following year, spring was full of contrasts. We left Gatwick in warm and brilliant sunshine to arrive in a cool, wet and very grey Toulouse. Philippe came to meet us. In spite of his knowing every short cut from airport to station we just missed the connection and by the time we reached the farm, it was late and still raining.

'You can't open up the house tonight,' said Claudette firmly. 'You must stay here.' The farmhouse was warm, the soup was gently bubbling on the stove and there was a *rôti* in the oven. We didn't argue.

In a chair in the corner, watched over by Grandma, sat a tired but contented Véronique with twelve-day-old Océane-Elodie in her arms. Océane, it seemed was the latest fashion in names. Elodie had been added to placate the priest who would christen her. Véronique explained that at one time all French babies had to be given the name of a saint which, I supposed, must account for the vast numbers of Anne-Maries and Jean-Pauls. At that moment, as if to prove it, Jean-Michel came striding in. He greeted us, then confidently took the baby, laying his cheek tenderly against hers. The likeness between them was already marked.

'Go and have a nap,' he said to his wife. 'I'll see to her.' It was clear that he was going to be an expert on babies as well as everything else.

We unloaded the various cheeses we had brought from England: Double Gloucester; Wensleydale; and Cornish Yarg, and unwrapped the selection of smoked fish from our favourite fishmonger. As if on cue Grandpa appeared, his nose already twitching.

'*Ah, bon, le poisson fumé,*' he smiled as he came to shake our hands.

'*Ça va Papi?*'

He shrugged. '*Oh … à mon âge … vous savez?*' But he didn't look any different. There was the sound of the returning tractor and a few moments later Raymond walked in, his face a little rounder and red with the rain.

'Ah, I see you've brought the rain with you,' he grinned.

'No,' we said. 'It was warm and sunny in England.'

'I don't believe it!'

During supper Raymond complained about the latest regulations from Brussels.

'I'm afraid this year Bel-Air won't be the house in the sunflowers,' he said.

I was disappointed for it was three years since we had had the joy of sunflowers in *le grand champ*, which stretches down towards the village.

'Why not?' I asked.

'New regulations,' he shrugged. 'First they encourage you – then it all changes.'

Now it seemed that in order to grow sunflowers he would have to leave fifteen per cent of his land *en jachère* – the dreaded set-aside.

'And, with all my animals, that's impossible,' he said.

With over sixty head of cattle he needs every available

meadow for both hay and, after the wheat, straw. Although I would miss the sunflowers I was glad not to be surrounded with sad fields of set-aside. Left to fill with thistles and other weeds when half the world is starving, they are a constant reproach. Certainly the local farmers, although not slow to appreciate being paid for doing nothing, prefer to see their fields full of a good crop of something edible. They have little time for *'les gens de Bruxelles'*. As Madame Barrou said to me recently:

'What do they know? *Les technocrates!* One came round to Monflanquin. He said to this farmer I know, *"Que c'est beau votre champ d'avoine."'* She grinned. *'Et vous savez ... c'était fèves!'* What a lovely field of oats – and you know what? – it was broad beans!

As far as Mme Barrou was concerned this summed up the entire Common Agricultural Policy.

We slept soundly that night on a soft bed with hard linen sheets and next morning Raymond took us up in the van to Bel-Air. It had stopped raining and the air smelled fresh and sweet. There were bright blue patches beginning to appear in the banks of racing clouds. The wheels churned up through the muddy track, and the path round the house was still lined with *nostoc commun*, green and slippery, but marguerites and love-in-a-mist bordered the meadow bright with buttercups.The cuckoo was loud in the wood and Claudette had already planted pansies in the pots on the porch. We were pleased to see that in each room there was a neat power plug. The electrician had worked well. We would be able to bring the word processor down in the summer and, more importantly at the moment, we could buy an electric fire. The most simple things which we take for granted in London are here a luxury and consequently much more appreciated.

After making the bed and unpacking we tried to start the 2CV which we keep in the barn next to the house. It is in fact Raymond's barn but as he only uses the middle section to store hay we make use of the rest of it. We bought the car second hand from Ruth Thomas when it became too small to transport her grandchildren, and it is a great favourite with my sons. It usually goes like the proverbial bomb. Today, however, it refused to start at all. Once more we were thankful for the telephone. M. Meunier, *le mécanicien*, said he would pop over after lunch; it was probably nothing serious. He was right. He simply pulled the rubber pipe off the carburettor, sucked hard, made a face as he spat out the petrol and quickly refixed the tube. The car started first try.

'I thought it was that,' he smiled. 'It's because it hasn't been used. You'll be able to do it yourself next time.'

Nicole, *la belle gymnaste*, was selling tickets for a dance to raise money for the tennis club. Mike is not keen on dancing but as Raymond is a marvellous dancer and quite capable of satisfying two partners I went with them. He has a natural sense of rhythm and can dance anything from a jive to a *paso doble*. It was just an ordinary country hop with children dashing about – such as one might find anywhere in England – except for the menu. There was a general scurrying back to the tables as the steaming tureens of soup were carried in. This was followed by salmon with an avocado sauce. Then we ate braised rabbit with vegetables. More bread was cut to mop up the gravy. The wine, the local *vin de table*, was unlimited. A delicious brie was followed by great slices of apple flan: and we'd only paid 100F each for the ticket.

We danced till 1.30 in the morning and then the good-byes were protracted. I didn't get much gardening done the next day but Raymond was up at his usual hour. Just before lunch he came round the side of the house carrying a sprouting conker. Its straight stem bore two bright little green leaves.

'*Regardez Ruth,*' he said. '*C'est joli.* Would you like it?' He held it tenderly in his rough, dirt-caked hands. 'But be careful where you plant it,' he smiled. 'It will grow very tall.' I foolishly put it in a pot until I could decide and, when we returned in the summer, it had dried out and died.

The day we arrived I was surprised to find a letter pushed underneath the front door. It was from an English woman who had enjoyed reading *House in the Sunflowers*.

'Oh yes,' said Raymond. 'I saw her come. She was on a horse,' he added.

'On a horse? What was she like?' He shrugged.

'Well – how old?'

He thought hard. *'Un certain âge,'* he said at last.

When I finally accepted her invitation and rang, the woman of *un certain âge* turned out to be seventy-seven. Not that anyone would guess. Ursula Hutchinson is remarkable, growing old extremely gracefully and making a happy life for herself in my part of France. British television has often of late shown programmes of English people living in France whose lives have gone from one disaster to another. Ursula's is a triumph. When her daughter and son-in-law and three of their seven children decided to come to France, Ursula thought that she too, would start a new phase in her life. She sold up, bought a rambling property with plenty of land for her two horses, and set about improving her French. She is slim and boyish with long legs and a wonderful grin. She is a great-grandmother and also the oldest woman competitor in endurance riding in France, and the corridor in her house is lined with rosettes. The last time I saw her she had recently celebrated her eightieth birthday and was at that moment in training for her next forty-kilometre ride that coming weekend.

Driving back from taking our student son to catch the London coach from Cahors, we later met another English couple making a great success of living in France. They had fallen in love with a derelict ironmongers-cum-junk-shop in the centre of Catus, a small town not far from Cahors. We too stopped in our tracks to look at this strange, balconied building, its walls painted with *fin-de-siècle* figures. The previous owner was Armand Lagaspie, poet, painter, and nightclub singer. He had lived much of his early life in Paris where he had illustrated the songs and poems of Aristide Bruant. Returning to Catus, he took over the family business which gradually changed from an ironmongers to a collection of anything which took his fancy. He lived to be ninety and kept a daily record of all the happenings in his town. When he died in 1963 he left everything to his daily help who was herself very old. On her death the place had to be sold, literally, lock and stock, if not barrel. Not many people were eager to take on this task but for Paul Garner and his partner Hazel, it was rather like us with Bel-Air – love at first sight, or, more dramatically in French – *un coup de foudre*. Since then they have spent many hours sorting out the contents and poring over old documents. Paul and Hazel, or Noisette as she is called by the locals, run an antique shop and small restaurant combined and are very happy. We were the only English people eating there that evening and have since taken Raymond and Claudette. The combination of good cooking preceded by browsing through second-hand bits and pieces is irresistible. If you are in luck you may even eat your meal to the strains of a pianola.

Our short spring holiday flew by. We made a quick trip to see M. Lecours. He had been too busy to start our roof but yes, he would definitely do it before we came back in July. As we had just paid the electrician we were quite glad that we didn't have to pay him as well. He promised to be as careful as possible with my plants round the house. I put little wigwams of sticks round the roses and the clematis and tied labels, saying *'Attention s'il vous plaît'*.

It was our last Sunday.

'Come down to lunch tomorrow,' said Claudette.

We protested. 'It's our turn.'

She shook her head. 'Philippe's friend will be here with his wife and little boy – the one he did his national service with – from l'île de la Réunion.' She laughed. 'You can't do lunch for fourteen and three babies. You'd never get them all in.'

It was true.

'Well, at least let me do the soup and the dessert?'

She reluctantly agreed and I set to work to make a great quantity of vichyssoise and then a tart with fresh oranges. It is a simple recipe but looks attractive and tastes wonderful. A square of thinly rolled out, puff pastry is pricked all over with a fork, leaving an inch border. A layer of marzipan laid on the pastry is then covered with fine, overlapping slices of thin-skinned oranges. When it is cooked the pastry rises round the edges to form a rim and the marzipan melts into the oranges. A quick glaze with melted apricot jam, a flash under the grill and it is ready.

It is quite a feat bumping down our track in a 2CV with a tureen of soup on one's lap, but it was eaten with relish. Then we all enjoyed the first asparagus of the season. Next came a *galantine de volaille* which was served with *mousserons*, then a green salad. Obviously Claudette had decided to make her usual rum baba whether or not I was going to bring a dessert. It was just as well. Although they loved the taste I was dismayed to see everyone of them carefully removing the peel from the orange slices. We are so used to eating marmalade it had never occurred to me that they might be reluctant to eat cooked orange peel.

We spent what was left of the afternoon sitting out in the courtyard in the spring sunshine admiring the children. Clément played with the three-year-old from the Island of Reunion, who was already learning English, and the new baby was passed from one to another.

It was an afternoon of celebrating new lives, while back in London, another life was coming to its untimely end. I had a message that evening to say that David's partner Charles had just died. I walked out by the pool where he had so enjoyed to swim. I remembered him as Matthew and I had last seen him in the London Lighthouse just before we came away. He was still very beautiful although incredibly thin and pale. His long hair cut because of the dreadful nightly sweats, he smiled, 'My mother has been longing for me to cut my hair for years.'

He was very calm and said that he was quite content because he had reached middle age. He was just thirty-five.

Towards the middle of June, Raymond rang us to tell us that M. Lecours had kept his word and had begun work on our roof. 'What is the weather like?' we asked, looking forward to leaving London as soon as we could.

'Perfect,' said Raymond. 'Hurry up and come!'

It was also perfect in July when we arrived, but everyone was still talking about the damage from the recent violent storm. There had been torrential rain and the local papers were full of pictures of disastrous flooding.

What about Bel-Air? 'You'd better cover your eyes,' said Grandma sadly as she handed us the key.

'Oh, we've swept out all the water,' said Raymond, but ...' he shrugged. He then explained that the storm couldn't have come at a worse moment. M. Lecours and his son had just finished taking all the tiles off the first section of the roof, which covered our bedroom with its pretty, new chestnut ceiling. Before leaving in the evening they had lashed down a tarpaulin which would normally have been sufficient to keep out any rain. No one had anticipated the strength of the storm or the hurricane force wind which, as well as blowing M. Lecour's tarpaulin away never to be found again, lifted whole rooves from barns and blew down trees and scaffolding. Hay crops had been ruined and vineyards all but destroyed. We drove up to Bel-Air not knowing what to expect.

It was a glorious afternoon. The grass was very long and everything looked well watered. M. Lecours and his son were on the roof, but it looked as though they had almost finished. An engine was chugging away and a small, very rusty crane towered over our house. Apart from a few broken tiles and chunks of cement in the flower beds it all looked its normal overgrown self. Inside it was a different story. There were long dirty streaks where the water had run down our bedroom walls and the ceiling was badly stained. All the grouting between the cream floor tiles was black and my white rugs were filthy. Fortunately I always cover the beds with plastic sheets before leaving and the brown stains trickling down them showed how necessary they had been. My heart sank at the hours of cleaning up there was to do. It seemed ironic that we had decided to have the roof done to prevent small leaks!

Luckily we had no visitors due for the next two weeks so the other bedrooms were free. We went outside and looked at the roof. The dips and sagging had all disappeared. The long slope of the roof was even and the cement edging was very neatly done. M. Lecours and his son took a break and came down to join us. They were very affable until, while discussing the storm damage, we casually mentioned the word insurance whereupon they became very sheepish and soon went back to work. The next day they both appeared side by side like a double act. They lit up and shuffled their feet. It would, they eventually said, puffing away, be far better if we were to claim on our insurance for the storm damage. We thought about it. It was clear that either they had no insurance or had forgotten to pay it; we would never know.

'We'd better decide what to say,' we said.

'You can say,' said M. Lecours, instantly more cheerful, 'that the wind blew off the ridge tiles and ... you had to get them replaced at once.'

'But won't he see that we've had the whole roof done?'

'Probably not. But if he does you can say that once we'd started it was clear that the whole roof needed doing.'

'Do you think he'll pay for a new chestnut ceiling?'

'Who knows? *On verra.*'

He wouldn't – of course. The insurance man was sympathetic. Yes, it had been a terrible storm. They would pay for new rugs and repairing the ridge tiles and for the chestnut ceiling to be sanded. M. Lecours laughed when he heard the last item. 'I'll give you a good estimate for that,' he said. 'I'd like to see him sanding a whole ceiling. It would break your arm.'

Having sanded a single beam I knew what he meant. I consoled myself with the thought of the insurance money as, on my hands and knees, I spent two days scrubbing each line of grouting between the floor tiles with bleach. The chestnut ceiling will never look the same. We have got used to it and now as the chestnut darkens with age the marks blend with the natural wood grain and are less worrying.

On Sunday Granny and Grandpa were going on a coach trip with the *troisième âge*, which meant that Raymond and Claudette were free. (I presume pensioners are called the third-agers because they are on their third score of years.) I had had a call from Sophie O'Neill, another successful transplant from England. She has an Anglo-French bookshop in the small town of Montcuq and had run out of copies of my book. A customer wanted to take one back to America the following week. Did I have some I could bring?

'Come on Sunday,' she had suggested. 'It's market day.'

It was a chance for us to take Raymond and Claudette out, something they always enjoy. We get a running commentary on every cultivated field we pass.

'Slow down, Michel,' Raymond will often shout in order to make a closer examination.

Montcuq was crowded. Not only was it market day; there was yet another market down under the trees, a once-a-year occasion. It was my first experience of *vider le grenier*. Like a car boot sale without the cars, it is literally 'empty the attic' day. I bought a very dirty, brass-framed, Moroccan mirror for 60 francs and we wished we had come earlier. Sophie O'Neill's shop was bright with fine watercolours her mother paints and full of French children buying and bringing her drawings they had done. She has fluent French, a very good range of new books and a flourishing second-hand section.

'Where can I take my neighbours for lunch?' I asked.

She smiled. 'Ah ... go to the Hotel de Quercy in Lauzerte,' she said. 'It's under new management. Don't be put off by the outside. It's quite shabby. But the food is by far the best around – and not expensive. You'd better book,' she added looking at her watch.

We telephoned from the shop, made our way to Lauzerte, a half-hour drive, and found a restaurant to which we have returned many times.

Lauzerte is a larger Bastide than Monflanquin. When we first saw it twenty years ago much of it was derelict. Now, in the summer months at least, it flourishes. People from many other parts of France as well as Americans, Dutch, and English have discovered its timeless beauty, poised high above a fertile plain. The Hotel de Quercy is not up in the trendy part of town. It sits, set back slightly from the road as it begins its steep climb. That first morning it certainly did not look very promising. Not at all the kind of place one would eagerly stop at for Sunday lunch except ... perhaps the more discerning traveller might sense the bustle and occasional glimpse of a white coat through an open door of the kitchen at the side. If the car window were open a waft of something delicious might alert the appreciative nose.

Up the steps, through the reception hall and into the

dining room, passing a table of patisseries and cold cabinet of desserts on the way, one's expectations begin to rise. The dining room is simple with no more than thirty covers. There is a real welcome from Mme Bacou and it is immediately clear that the chef is not content with a run-of-the-mill menu. As we began to read Raymond looked very worried but Claudette was excited. I think we ate the 90 F menu that day. I remember that after the soup we began with a galantine of sweetbreads with raisins which absolutely melted in the mouth. Then we all chose something different and tasted each others dishes. I had turbot on a bed of wild rice with an assortment of vegetables and after the cheese, a charlotte du Cointreau with bitter oranges. Even Raymond was won over by the end of the meal. It was all as beautifully arranged as the most expensive nouvelle cuisine but happily, more copious. People in this part of France have hearty appetites.

The wine we chose was a Cahors from the Château de Brel de Fargues and it was so good that after lunch we got out the map and went for a *dégustation.* This is quite a popular Sunday afternoon activity and it is hard to find anywhere more attractive than the rolling vineyards of the Lot Valley. Cahors vineyards are among the oldest in France, dating back to the Roman occupation. The dark wine of Cahors was adopted by the Greek Orthodox Church as its communion wine and it was chosen to be served to distinguished visitors by the Tsars of Russia. As other regions began to prosper it fell out of favour and many vineyards were completely destroyed by the frosts of 1956. Now, largely thanks to M. Pompidou, it is making a deserved comeback. It is made with a mixture of Merlot, Tannat and Auxerrois grapes, the latter giving it its distinctive bite.

La patronne at the Château de Brel made us welcome and explained that they age their wine *en fut* – in the barrel – for two years, before bottling. We bought a few bottles and then Raymond started off on a quest to find a certain wine producer that he had known as a child.

'It's called Domaine de Lavergne,' he said. 'It's got to be somewhere round here.' He told us of trips years ago with his uncle to fetch more of a very special Cahors to top up *la perpétuelle*. *Une perpétuelle*, he explained, was a smaller barrel which was put down at the birth of a child. After a certain time a little would be drawn off each year and some more added. In this way it never got too old but never tasted new. After many detours with Raymond turning his head from side to side and squinting up at the hillsides he suddenly shouted '*C'est là!*' Sure enough at the top of the lane was the sign. Lavergne.

A dog barked furiously as we approached. It did not look very promising but eventually, a woman with rough grey hair and a weather-beaten face silenced the dog and came down the steps to meet us. She turned out to be the daughter-in-law of the former patron who Raymond had known. 'A*h oui, le Pépé,*' she said sadly. '*Il est mort – mais –* how kind he always was.'

She began to reminisce about those early days. Originally from Italy, she had found life hard when she first came, having to learn how to tie all the grafts with raffia. 'But *le Pépé* – he would always show me the best way to do everything, to avoid aches and pains, you understand.'

She led us into the cave which was very small and cool. Raymond sighed and looked round nostalgically.

'We keep our wine five years *en fut* before bottling,' she told us.

'Do you still have the wonderful stuff we used to come up here for? *Pour la perpétuelle. Vous en avez encore?*' asked Raymond.

She smiled, shook her head and tapped the side of her nose.

'*Pour la famille, Monsieur – vous comprenez.*'

'*Bien sûr*,' said Raymond, regretfully.

She talked about the visiting wine experts and their advice. 'My son says we have to listen, but ... all this *filtrage*. As far as I'm concerned all the wine in the valley tastes the same. But up here, on the hillside ... it's still got that special difference.'

It was certainly very good with the distinctive tang of Cahors and we bought a case each. She gave us a complimentary bottle of the previous year and we took a glass of ratafia which she told us was unfermented grape juice mixed with *eau-de-vie*.

'*Vous vendangez avec les machines?*' asked Raymond. She shook her head.

'All by hand, monsieur. The whole family and all our friends.'

She smiled up at him showing several gaps in her teeth.

As we drove away Raymond shook his head. 'She used to be so beautiful.' he said.

'*Eh, mon ami!*' laughed Claudette. 'How long ago?'

'Forty years at least,' said Raymond with a wry smile.

As we drove home Raymond talked again about planting vines in the field below the wood.

'You'd be able to see them from your front door.' he said.

This would at least partly make up for the demise of the sunflowers, I agreed, but it seemed that there might still be intervention from the dreaded bureaucrats. Permission had to be granted by the Bureau de Viticulture at Bordeaux.

'It's not easy,' said Raymond. 'They're very strict.'

He told us that he had already been refused once but a certain nursery man he knew who sold vines and was on the board of the bureau – or as Raymond put it, '*il est comme chez lui là-bas*', – was going to put in a word for him.

'As he told them,' said Raymond proudly, 'my friend takes all his grapes to the *Cave des Sept Monts* at Monflanquin and they are improving their wine every year now. Remember ... they've already won several medals at Paris. This is just the sort of conscientious producteur that we must encourage.'

'So, you really think you'll get permission?'

'*Sans doute,*' said Raymond happily.

'*Encore du travail*' – more work, said Claudette, raising her eyebrows.

It was the end of the first week of *Musique en Guyenne* in Monflanquin and there was a free concert of excerpts in the square. We were back in time to listen. Instrumental pieces by Gershwin and Mendelssohn were followed by one item from the choir. This year they were over a hundred strong and of eleven different nationalities. The final concert this season was to be a performance of Handel's *Messiah*. Sent the music to learn at the beginning of the year and only coming together two weeks before the final concert, it inevitably takes several rehearsals to make an integrated sound. They ended this evening's appetiser by singing the Hallelujah chorus. The audience wouldn't let them go until they had sung it three times and, happily, they got better each time.

At the final concert of the whole work in the church on the following Sunday, the improvement was marked. This was an inspired and disciplined choir and the soloists were magnificent, especially the English soprano Judith Howarth. She sang as if illuminated and the packed church breathed with her. The young orchestra from Westphalia played as brilliantly as always under the baton of a conductor who might have been drawn by Ralph Steadman, and the applause at the end went on and on. People were genuinely moved.

Still in a daze, we came out into the night. It was very warm. Most of the audience went straight home but I needed time to recover. We sat in a café and ate ice-cream. Some of the young musicians came to say goodbye to the jovial patron. We had often seen them during the week eating great pizzas and mountains of chips. But they could not stay now as the coach was waiting to take them straight back to Germany that same night.

The patron hugged them. *'A l'année prochaine, hein?'* he said, pinching their cheeks. 'Play something,' he pleaded suddenly. One of them took out his trumpet, walked to the end of the stone arcade and began. The sound was clear and haunting and, in the stillness, made a moment of inexplicable sadness, before they all hugged him again, waved, picked up their instruments and ran to catch the coach. Not for the first time we thought how lucky we were as we drove home beneath a sky full of stars.

16

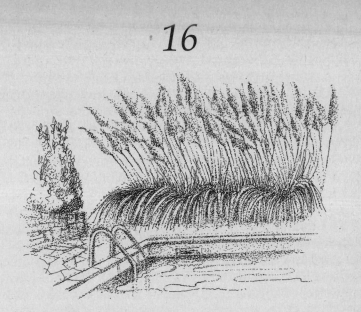

We gave a fresh lick of paint to our bedroom walls before the first of the family arrived. Matthew, our younger son, had hardly recovered from the journey when he was persuaded by Philippe and the other young people to go to the large nightclub on the other side of Villeneuve. With lasers sweeping across the sky it is a focal point for the young at the weekend. Clément and Océane were left with their maternal grandmothers while their parents went off to dance the night away, Corinne's brother gallantly acting as chauffeur. No stranger to London nightlife, Matthew was surprised, not at the high price of the drinks, but at the fact that they appeared to be sold by the bottle. Most of the young, dressed in their very best clothes, seemed to pool their money on arriving. There was no pouring of drinks at the bar. A fistful of crumpled notes were exchanged for a fistful of glasses, a bottle of whisky, gin or vodka. Véronique had been to watch Johnny Halliday who was apparently celebrating his fiftieth birthday with a nationwide tour, and she joined them afterwards. They all got home at 5 a.m. Matthew collapsed into bed but Phillippe, after coffee and cognac, went fishing with Jean-Michel. He seems to have inherited his father's stamina.

A few days later we were down at the farm after supper and just about to leave when news of the arrival of hundreds of shooting stars that very night was announced on television.

'Don't go to bed,' said the eager young announcer. 'Switch off all the lights. Take a deckchair into the garden and wrap yourself in an eiderdown. Lie back and watch *les étoiles filantes*.'

The shooting stars were apparently the debris from a collision of two stars many years before. The night sky at Bel-Air is always magical and it seemed a pity to miss this, perhaps once in a lifetime, free spectacle. It was still warm but we took blankets and lay on the recliners by the pool. It was very dark, we were very tired and nothing much happened before midnight. Just as we were thinking of giving up, thin threads of brilliant light began to arc from every direction. It was amazing. We stopped saying 'There's another one,' and just watched. There are no lights anywhere near us and, in the intense darkness, the effect was like some silent, awesome firework display. The climax was to be around 3 a.m. but by one o'clock Mike and I gave up. Matthew set his alarm, had an hour's sleep and got up again to watch the grand finale, with the moon coming up to join the show.

In Monflanquin banners in blue and yellow were appearing as everyone prepared for the *Fête Médiévale*. *Les Monflanquinois* are very aware and very proud of their history. This is due in no small measure to M. George Odo, who is a passionate historian, and lives in the town. He writes and gives wonderful lectures which vividly recreate the life of this small Bastide town in the Middle Ages. Most

170

of the activity for the Fête takes place in the market square, first measured out in 1252, after the land was formally ceded to one Alphonse de Poitiers, the king's brother. The market is still held to this day on a Thursday, as it was then decreed. The inspiration for the layout of these Bastides went back to antiquity – to the simplest plan of a Roman city. The word 'bastide' came from the Occitan, 'bastida' – a group of buildings, or even a construction site. Their most important feature was the market place. Neither the church nor the dwelling of a nobleman was allowed to dominate the town. Access had to be controlled so that outsiders would be forced to pay dues, for the object was to collect taxes from both those inside and outside. Alphonse de Poitiers was eventually responsible for the founding of fifty-seven new towns, or Bastides, in all.

These new towns were part of a general growth of population and trade in thirteenth century Europe, but in France, they were also the solution to a particular problem. Many areas in the south had been ravaged in the brutal extermination of the Cathars, those followers of a heretical religion which had come across from Eastern Europe. At a time when the established church was very corrupt, these new priests, or *parfaits*, as they were called, had a strong appeal for simple people. The war against them, backed by the threatened church, had been merciless. Now it was necessary to regroup all those peoples dispersed in the fighting. Also in the constant war against the English, who ruled over Aquitaine, the French crown had always been conscious of the need to gain more power in the south-west. To this end, Alphonse de Poitiers had been married to the daughter of the *Comte de Toulouse* at the age of nine and in 1249 he inherited his lands. As soon as he returned from a crusade he started his great building project, Monflanquin being given its charter in 1256.

Alphonse, apparently always in debt, took his revenue three times a year. In 1268, 140 livres were raised in

Monflanquin. Three years later the sum had risen to 200 livres and the new town was flourishing, but Alphonse himself died that same year.

Eighteen years later Monflanquin was part of the English kingdom and Edward I decided to fortify the town. He finished building the arcades which still surround the square and was responsible for the construction of four great gateways and ramparts with eleven towers which, unfortunately, would be pulled down much later on the orders of Cardinal Richelieu. In spite of Edward's strong defences, the town was soon retaken by the French. However, within ten years it was again English and much of the revenue now came in very useful to pay for the war against Scotland.

In all these changes the local people did not take sides. As far as the *Monflanquinois* were concerned, the northern French and English were equally foreign for neither spoke the *Langue d'Oc*, the language of the south. But amongst the townspeople, with their carefully drawn-up charters of rights and responsibilities, there was a new spirit abroad. A sense of civic pride and independence was born, which has never quite disappeared. Until 1950 many of the families in Monflanquin were descended directly from those who had lived there since the Middle Ages. The *Fête Médiévale*, although primarily a device to promote tourism, is planned with a historian's help and has its roots very firmly in the past.

It gets more ambitious every year. On the Sunday morning the square is full of craftsmen demonstrating ancient crafts. They make barrels, weave baskets and splice ropes while jugglers, fire-eaters and acrobats enthrall the children. Dmitri, staff in hand, walks slowly round with his three brown bears. He is part of a group of travelling musicians from Romania. Although both my conscience and my reason tell me that I should disapprove of the bears, I still find myself completely fascinated by them.

Attached to his wide leather belt they lumber along at his side, licking his arms and stopping to munch the odd apple. They are huge, with fearsome claws. They lift their great heads and look at the humans.

One of the narrow alleys which run between the backs of the houses is strewn with straw, and children ride on a donkey between the perambulating chicken. In the evening there will be musicians. Various folkloric groups in costume sing and play on old instruments.

We came late one evening. I thought at first that the musicians really needed a microphone to carry the sound over the still chattering crowd, in shorts and tee-shirts, who sat idly watching them, their cameras slung over their shoulders. But as it got darker and modern ears slowly adjusted, the square gradually fell silent. It was strange how hypnotic the monotonous music became. The beat of the drum and the squeak of the primitive cornet worked their magic. The singers were harsh and strident. They sang of battles, of unrequited love, and of treachery. There was a wonderful ballad about a rat-king and, suddenly, there he was in the square with a thick tail two metres long. And as he turned, the children screamed, jumping over the snaking, swirling tail. We took up the refrain or began to clap our hands. In the dim light in the ancient square, the twentieth century disappeared, and faces took on a simple, timeless wonder.

On the last night of the fête there is a colourful banquet – as many people as possible dressed in medieval costume. All our young people went, and that year three whole pigs were roasted. We arrived late with Raymond and Claudette who were looking after the baby. It was almost eleven o'clock before we pushed Océane in her pram into the square to join the others. Three-year-old Clément was still hopping about. We were just in time to see the town council, beautifully robed, dancing a stately pavane all round the square. They had apparently been practising for weeks. They obviously enjoyed it so much that every time there was a lull in the proceedings, up they got and started again. I felt I would never view the local Doctor, the schoolmaster or Madame in the tourist bureau in quite the same way again.

More friends and family arrived and soon we were *complet* – even the camp site. When he wasn't in the pool, Thomas, my grandson, now two-and-a-half, spent a great deal of time looking for tigers in the head-high maize, hotly pursued by one of us before he got completely lost. We had great alfresco meals with everyone contributing dishes. Kate's barbecued bananas flambéed in Armagnac were a real success.

Raymond brought Clément up to play with Thomas.

'*Regarde, Clément! C'est Thomas, ton petit copain,*' he said eagerly. They eyed each other warily and clung to their respective toys. We all sang Frère Jacques together and they giggled. Gradually they got used to each other and raced about with a fire engine apiece yelling 'Nee-naw. Nee-naw!' – that being much the same in any language.

On Sunday we all ate at the farm and during the meal found the two little boys sitting side by side on the step of the cow byre. They had managed to lift the heavy latch and open the door but as the massive beasts turned their heads to look at them they hesitated to go in. Later they came round the corner in guilty glee having picked two green lemons from Claudette's tree. Feeding the ducks and hens was their favourite pastime. They each sat on a brick in the yard with a small tin of corn to throw and were soon surrounded by a wonderful variety of birds.

A week later there was a sudden heavy downpour and Mike went up in the attic to make sure that there were no leaks. It was bone-dry but he noticed that the crack, which had always been there, between the chimney and the wall, had widened. We mixed a bucket of cement and collected a few stones but, when we began to work we realised that the crack went deeper than we had thought. More alarmingly than that, through the gap we could see the end of a rafter which appeared to protrude into the chimney itself and was badly charred. We decided it might be prudent to call M. Duparcq.

He was his usual lugubrious self. He nodded calmly. *'Oui, c'était souvent comme ça.'* With a total disregard for any fire risk, it was apparently quite common in very old houses not to bother to cut off the tip of the end rafter, but to leave it in the chimney. Up in the attic M. Duparcq sawed away and, with a shout of *'Attention!'*, the piece landed in the hearth. It was as hard and black as a lump of coal and, had we known it was there, would have terrified us every time we lit the fire. He filled the crack in the attic and then came downstairs. To Thomas's delight he then put a ladder in the hearth and, to fill the crack from the inside, he disappeared up the wide chimney. Ever after he was known to Thomas as the Grand old Duke of Parcq who, when he was only half way up etc ...

My hedge of pampas grass that protected the pool from the east was splendid this year. The clumps are fascinating to watch in the summer as the plumes gradually emerge from their thick green sheaths. First there is just the hint of a silver pen nib, the next day and the day after they are like flat edged paintbrushes, then they push up and begin to open. Taller and taller and more and more beautiful, they look fully gown until you examine them more closely, then you find that there are still another few inches to come before the silver plumes finally stand clear and move in the sunlight. I counted over a hundred that summer. Fortunately they do not shed their seeds until the middle of October when the pool is covered for the winter.

It was time for the family to leave. My older son Adam had a lighting project in Dubai and Matthew had decided to go back to college. On their last night, Thomas and I sat by the pond to see the sun go down over the edge of the world. Later he watched the moon come up and he sang 'Twinkle twinkle little star' to a sky full of stars, and I wondered if he would remember any of it when he was older.

In spite of the storms in June the plum harvest was not as bad as expected. The maize cut, Raymond began once again to think about the new vineyard.

'Have you got your permission yet?' we asked.

'*Non*,' he replied. 'But it's only a question of time.'

We sat on the porch looking up towards the wood. A new calf had just been born in the field, a female. Raymond was pleased. Already she was standing, snatching vigorously at the udder, the umbilical cord still dangling from her belly. The day before we left Raymond was triumphant. Permission had at last been granted: we would have a new vineyard. Grandpa sniffed and said nothing but Jean-Michel, as he ate his soup with one hand and nursed the baby on his shoulder, gave a confident grin.

'*C'est bien!*' he said.

17

It was at the beginning of January that Claudette phoned us in London.

'Are you doing anything special the week of February 21st? she asked.

'No,' we said, intrigued. Claudette never phones without a purpose.

'Well – you see – it's just possible that Véronique may be able to take a week's holiday and she could look after Granny and Grandpa and – if she can – and if we can get a cheap flight – but it's not certain you understand ...'

We assured them of their permanent welcome and scribbled the date in our diaries; perhaps this time they really would be able to come.

Claudette had been for a brief weekend years ago, when Philippe, then fourteen, had first stayed with Matthew. Raymond, although always intending to visit London, had never managed it. He always talks with such pleasure about the few brief holidays he has had, when he has been able to leave the farm. He has spent the odd weekend in Paris and he is an enthusiastic sightseer. We knew he would find London exciting.

So many times we had said when crossing Waterloo bridge at night, as we admire the lighted buildings on either side reflected in the gleaming water, 'How Raymond would enjoy this.' As we stood on the balcony outside the Festival Hall in the interval of a concert and gazed across the river, looking at the varied skyline with the illuminated curves of the new Charing Cross station, we would repeat, 'Raymond would love this.' But with a mixed farm, with over sixty head of cattle to be cared for, and ageing parents, it never seemed to be the right moment to leave. Now, with an ever confident Jean-Michel, things were changing. Perhaps they really would make it.

Meanwhile I was deep in the throes of editing a play for a projected reading at the Theatre Museum in Covent Garden in three weeks time. Rewriting, finding twelve actors generous enough to give me a whole day, sending out invitations, compiling a programme and a part for a narrator – not to mention twisting my agent's arm to direct it for me – I must admit that Raymond and Claudette faded into the background. But once the reading was successfully over and we began to recover, we wondered if they would indeed come. We heard nothing. The weeks passed. On the Friday evening before the proposed visit we happened to look at the diary.

'What a shame,' I said.

'I never really thought they would manage it,' said Mike. 'There's always some last minute crisis.'

'Perhaps we'd just better phone,' I said. 'To make absolutely certain.'

'They would surely have been in touch before now if they were coming,' said Mike as he dialled.

'*Mais si!*' Raymond shouted excitedly. 'I was going to call you on Saturday. We shall be at – ' eventually we realised that it was 'Heathrow' he was trying to say, 'at 8.40 on Monday morning.'

We spent the next two days cancelling appointments, spring-cleaning the guest room, trying to plan a programme and most important of all, shopping for food! At last they were really coming to London.

Being certain to reach Heathrow by 8.40 on a Monday morning meant getting up soon after six. We were somewhat bleary-eyed as we waited at the barrier, watching the passengers from the flight from Toulouse filing out. Some were instantly greeted by friends and there was a great deal of kissing. Neat businessmen in unmistakably French suits searched for strangers carrying pieces of cardboard with company labels. Children were re-united with parents. The flow of passengers became a trickle then stopped. Where were our intrepid pair? Was it possible, after all our frantic preparations, that they had missed the plane?

We hovered, uncertain what to do. But, at last our stragglers emerged, Raymond in an elegant jacket, Claudette following in a full skirt, little Victorian boots and a jaunty cap. She threw up her hand in a characteristic gesture.

'*On a eu un petit désastre*,' she cried.

They were full of apologies. Apparently in one of their soft-topped suitcases they had unwisely packed several bottles of wine, one of which had broken.

'The best one, of course,' cursed Raymond.

'That's why we're so late,' explained Claudette. 'It was all over the carousel. We had to mop it up and throw the pieces of glass away.'

I wondered if anyone else had found their suitcases soaked in *vin de pays de l'Agenais*, but I didn't enquire as we sped towards the centre of London, the car smelling like the *Cave Co-opérative* at Monflanquin.

It was a rare, glorious February morning and wisely we

decided to make the most of it with a quick tour of London. Raymond 'oohed' and 'aahed' at the white stucco buildings of Kensington and Park Lane and, as we crossed and recrossed the Thames in brilliant sunlight, at Big Ben, Parliament Square, Buckingham Palace and Victoria. Everything did look impressive, especially the river. Raymond was as enchanted as we had hoped.

That night we took them to the Festival Hall. From our favourite seats in the choir they enjoyed the London Philharmonic playing Tchaikovsky and Sibelius and, in the interval, did indeed exclaim at the view from the balcony. Raymond also exclaimed next morning at the sight of six fat pigeons on my lawn.

'*Regarde! Claudette, regarde!*' he shouted, leaping up from the table.

'*Mais ... c'est pas des pigeons – c'est des poules – oh là!*'

He decided that the first thing he needed on this holiday was a map. 'Then I shall learn all about London,' he declared optimistically.

The sunshine of the previous day did not reappear for the rest of the week but nothing could dampen Raymond's enthusiasm. Map in hand we began with a visit to the Museum of London and as we later climbed the steps of St Paul's it began to snow. That evening I cooked baked gammon with parsley sauce, jacket potatoes and lots of vegetables. Raymond would have none of the sauce.

'*Gôute-là, au moins,*' pleaded Claudette. At least try it.

But he enjoyed the meat and ate half a loaf with the vegetables, and the other half with the cheese and apple crumble.

On the following morning I had an engagement that I had been unable to cancel, so Mike thought that they might enjoy a trip to Harrod's food hall. Apart from the shock of finding *foie gras* from Germany on sale, this visit turned out to be one of the highlights of their trip. Before they set out Mike was rather surprised when Raymond asked if he might borrow a briefcase; not exactly something one would normally associate with Raymond. It was soon apparent however, that this visit to London was not to be all pleasure and sightseeing. As Raymond loaded a pile of leaflets and brochures for *France Prune* and *la Cave des Sept Monts* into the briefcase he explained that he also saw his visit as an opportunity *'de faire un peu de publicité pour notre région'*.

As they left for Harrods, Mike, all too aware that he lacked any skill as a commercial traveller, but that he would have, inevitably, to act as interpreter, wondered just what lay ahead.

In the food hall they marvelled at the variety of foods, and hunted high and low until they found, at last, *les pruneaux d'Agen.* But they were horrified at the price. Now all they had to do, said Raymond, was to persuade Harrods to buy them from their local co-operative. Mike had no choice. After several deep breaths he found a sympathetic sales assistant and explained the situation, Raymond beaming encouragingly. Next Mike spoke on the telephone to the assistant buyer, translating all the while to an eager and anxious Raymond. He explained that without an appointment it wasn't possible to meet a buyer, nor without the previous sending of samples. Raymond shrugged and pulled a face. But they would be very happy to see some brochures. A triumphant Raymond fished in his briefcase and handed them over and Mike thanked the assistant and heaved a sigh of relief.

'Très bien,' cried Raymond flushed with success. 'Now, Michel, we must find the wine buyer!' And it began all over again.

When I joined them later my husband looked a little weary. Raymond was in fine form. He had left wine brochures in a branch of Oddbins, and in Harrods. In a local shop, while trying to buy *les puddings de Noël*, as presents for the family, they had actually found prunes from their own co-operative. Later Mike described to me his experiences in Marks and Spencers in Chelsea, where Raymond had, at first been unable to find any dried fruit at all. On enquiring, an assistant had led them to a less than prominent position. Raymond had clapped his hand to his head. 'You must tell her, Michel,' he said 'they'll never sell them here! They need to be properly displayed. Over there in the centre!'

In the afternoon we went to Kenwood, where old friends, Pauline and Ip Wong were there to meet us. Their son Yan had stayed on to help Raymond with the plum harvest the previous year before going up to Oxford. Unfortunately our journey was held up by a demonstration by impoverished and disaffected students and by the time we arrived the house was shut. Undaunted, Raymond and Claudette enjoyed looking with farmer's eyes at Capability Brown's garden, even in February. We had a drink at the Spaniard's Inn and then Ip cooked a Chinese meal. Raymond struggled manfully with *les baguettes* – chopsticks – but, like me, soon gave up. As all the food was unfamiliar he was more or less forced to try very small portions of everything but his worried look soon vanished and he came back for more – and more. Claudette wanted to buy 'typically English' presents and in a sudden flash of inspiration Pauline remembered the National Trust shop in the old Bluecoat School building near Victoria. It was very quiet and stuffed with just the sort of thing Claudette was looking for.

Unfortunately *les Fostaires* were away but other mutual friends joined us for supper the next day and we cooked an enormous dish of mussels and ate cold ham and chicken with various salads. Claudette was very intrigued with sticky toffee pudding and demanded the recipe. Raymond was very anxious to see an English farm, not easy in Clapham. Had we had more notice of their coming we would have been able to arrange it, as it was we just pointed the car next morning towards Kent and set off.

It was a grey, bleak day. We passed one or two large and

prosperous farmhouses and Raymond seemed perplexed when we did not immediately turn into the drive.

'Isn't that a farm there?' he cried.

'Yes, perhaps, but ...'

'Aren't English farmers very welcoming then?' he asked in some surprise.

We were saved from having to try to explain by the sound of a tractor. In the next gateway an old bent man gave us a wave. I squelched across the yard followed by an eager Raymond and the next half hour was spent by two farmers happily cursing both arthritis and the bureaucrats in Brussels in equal measure, while Claudette, who had borrowed Véronique's Camcorder, filmed a beautiful herd of Jersey cows. The old man was the farm manager for a widow with two sons, neither of whom wanted to be farmers: Raymond was sympathetic.

We had a pub lunch later at the Henry the Eighth at Hever where Raymond was horrified to find his baguette already buttered. He scraped off the butter as carefully as if it had been arsenic. According to Raymond, a real man of the South, it is the wretched and much disliked Normans who started the spreading of butter on everything.

'*Comme il est difficile!*' sighed Claudette. 'They were just trying to do a bit of publicity for their region,' we teased him.

Adam got us tickets to see *Les Miserables* that evening. It was a spectacular production and we thought that at least they would know the story. On the following morning my cousin David and his mother took them to Kew to see the millions of crocuses, which were donated by Reader's Digest. Claudette sighed at the camellias in bud and wished she could have come when they were in flower. We had lunch in the orangery and spent the rest of the afternoon in the various glass houses, Claudette filming away and Raymond darting from one plant to another demanding translations.

183

'Claudette, regarde!' he cried. *'C'est la plante qui donne le café!'* He was fascinated. He had drunk it every day of his life but this was the first time he had ever seen it growing.

On Sunday he wanted to go to Mass in an Anglican church. 'As I am in England, I want to see how they do it, *les Anglicans,'* he said. We took them to Southwark Cathedral. They were most impressed with the unhurried dignity of it all, the beauty of the singing, and not least by the serving of both bread and wine at the communion. I have found that the further south one goes in Europe the faster and more crowded the Mass becomes, but I have never seen the wine served.

Raymond had insisted on buying an English gigot for the Sunday meal. We had to compromise between serving it practically raw, as he likes it, and just pink for everyone else. Claudette got busy in the kitchen making *un flan.* We had more discussion about the difference between English and French ovens but she was very impressed with my eye-level grill, something she had never seen before.

While we were cooking, my sons took Raymond for a drink at the Windmill on Clapham Common. Before we all sat down to eat Claudette took cuttings of everything in sight and Raymond pruned the fruit trees in my garden and my son Adam's. After this last meal with all the family, we marked everywhere that we had been on Raymond's map. The next morning we were up early to take them to the airport. We were exhausted, but we were equally glad to have been able to return just a fraction of their wonderful hospitality. We could never repay the kindness they have shown us since that afternoon when we took our first drink together to celebrate signing the contract to buy Bel-Air.

18

It was April. We had arrived that afternoon and were all having supper together. Claudette had made sorrel soup followed by an asparagus omelette, and a quiche filled with cauliflower. Raymond was complaining about his knee.

'I don't understand it,' he said. 'The cow was giving birth and she kicked me hard. Here!' He rubbed his buttock. 'But it's my knee that is swollen. Look. *C'est vraiment bizarre.*'

'It's already better than yesterday,' said Claudette briskly.

Raymond seemed doubtful, but took another helping of quiche.

As we then tucked into home potted pork with salad, Grandpa, who had looked at Raymond's knee without comment, told us about the excellent meal that the *troisième âge* had recently enjoyed at a local restaurant.

'*La soupe était extra,*' he said solemnly. 'Just like Claudette makes.'

He paused; we waited. '*Et ... après,*' ... he lifted his head and made sure we were all listening ... *'un très bon hors-d'oeuvre avec de tout* ... gizzards, duck breast, tomatoes and olives. *Après ... une galantine de volaille avec une sauce, et puis ... brochette de canard ... fromage ... tourtière*. All for 120F. *Le vin rosé* wasn't up to much,' he added, with a touch of his usual asperity. 'But,' he nodded ... *'le repas était copieux.'*

Grandma agreed. How she got through it all with her sparrow's appetite I can't imagine. Grandpa took another slice of bread and chuckled.

'Ah oui,' he said. 'She was trying to get her reputation back – *la Patronne.* She knew she had overcharged for the champagne at our New Year celebrations!'

Le troisième âge it seemed, still wielded some power.

Raymond talked of his trip to London. He got out his map to show Grandpa the places he had visited.

'And, you know,' he said, 'I didn't dare put my briefcase down – in case they thought it was a bomb.'

The next morning, after a quick trip to the supermarket, we started on the garden. That was what we really came for on these short trips in spring. After the waist-high grass, the next job was the cutting of last year's plumes on the pampas grasses. They were too beautiful to cut when we left in the autumn. We were not here in December, the best time for pruning, so they were by now a sorry, bedraggled sight. Although the temperature was already in the mid-seventies during the day, for this task covered arms and legs were a necessary protection against the razor-like edges of the leaves. It took all day, as I loaded and reloaded the wheelbarrow. But I found a use for the strongest canes as supports for my morning glories and canary creepers. The buddleia bush seemed to have survived, and the canna lilies that I had planted the previous summer were just poking through a thick layer of bark chippings.

Raymond, in spite of the knee, was working in the orchard with Jean-Michel. As a precaution against any high winds this summer, they were putting a strong wooden support against every tree. Evidence of Jean-Michel was all around. Fences were mended – an eternal task – and there were new stalls for another six young bulls.

By nine thirty that evening it was still 72° on the porch. The croaking of frogs both in the pond and under the edge of the pool cover, was deafening as each group answered the other. A thin layer of mist began to roll up from the south, as though someone had teased out a long strand of cotton wool and placed it with great care between the horizon and the nearest band of trees.

All week we worked in the garden. It was wonderfully therapeutic. When we left London, I had been in the middle of writing a children's story, but had lost inspiration. I can recommend a week's gardening for writer's block. It is such hard physical work that the only possible imagining is imagining what it all might look like in three month's time. It worked wonders for me and I spent the evenings scribbling away.

On Sunday it was the first of May and the *Fête des Fleurs* at the nearby town of Tournon d'Agenais. Another thirteenth century Bastide, the whole hilltop town was that day like a miniature Chelsea Flower Show. Every nursery-man throughout the south-west had been given a section of the town in which to set up his garden display. Claudette was in her element and we were soon loaded with plants, but Raymond spent most of the time sitting down on the nearest bench. His knee, which had been much better, was swollen again. They had been to the tennis dance the previous night. I had been too tired to join them.

'What time did you get in?' I asked.

'Three a.m.' said Raymond. *'Mais – c'est pas ça.'* He shook his head, then grinned sheepishly. *'J'ai trop dansé le cha cha cha.'*

He cheered up as we set off for the Hotel de Quercy at Lauzerte for another marvellous meal and, on the way, talked about his dilemma of whether or not to sell some of his maize to the co-operative. In spite of the early storms the previous June, it had been a bumper harvest. His silo was full but he might run out and need more. It was possible to sell with the understanding that, if you needed to, you could buy some back again. Then what was the problem?

'It won't necessarily be my own maize,' said Raymond.

I smiled. '*Non, non,*' he protested. 'They might give me kiln dried – it's not nearly so good. Mine, you know, is dried *au naturel.*'

Now I understood. Raymond still dries his maize in a crib. It is halfway down our track and we must pass it every day; a wire cage on stilts, about 100 feet long and 15 feet high, and very narrow, to ensure the maximum penetration of sunlight and air. These cribs straddle the countryside and when full of golden cobs they glow in the sunlight.

On Monday morning he was back in the orchard, this time wearing the special protective headgear which makes him look like a deep-sea diver, as he sulphated the trees against carpocapse, a particularly virulent pest. This task completed, he asked if Mike would help him measure out the field below the wood which was to become the new vineyard. 'I'm not sure exactly how many vines I have room for,' he said.

The field was bright with buttercups.

'They look pretty but they're no good for the hay,' said Raymond as they trudged off, each with a bamboo cane three metres long. I cut last year's dried tansy stalks and put them in a basket for kindling, while the two men paced back and forth over the meadow. When they returned, hot and thirsty, we sat together under the porch. Raymond looked uneasy.

After measuring it seemed that they would need 3100 stakes, one for each vine. Raymond scratched his head. '3100! I'm a bit scared. It's not easy planting a new vineyard.'

He then explained the complications that he had already had to go through with *Le Bureau de Viticulture* in Bordeaux. The famous permission, which he had eventually been granted by dint of persuasion by his influential friend, the nurseryman, had only been the first part of the process. He then learned that no new licences were being issued. Before he could buy his new vines, he must first buy up old licences from vineyards which were being discontinued.

'*Oui,*' said Raymond. '*Tout ce que j'avais – c'était le droit d'acheter les autres droits!* Permission to buy other permits. *C'est tellement compliqué!*'

To make it even more *compliqué*, to buy these unwanted licences, he was in competition with *Le Bureau* itself who, wishing to get rid of small, inferior vineyards would pay about 20000F *per hectare* – almost two-and-a-half acres.

'But that's a fortune,' I said.

He smiled. 'Oh I didn't pay that. To get the full price, *la prime d'arrachage*, you must sell immediately. If you hang on until you make up your mind whether or not to replant, the Bureau are not interested and the price goes down all the time. When you buy from a small *producteur*, the going rate is about 3000F *l'hectare* – I bought 19 here, 30 there. I asked around you see. If you don't replant within seven years the permit expires and is worthless. Time passes and people forget. Mind you, they are getting more expensive. The last lot I bought – the old woman said 3000F on the phone, but when I got there, it was already 4000F. Good job I didn't wait a week.'

'But I still don't understand why they don't all sell to the Bureau?' I asked.

'Oh – you know – they're not too keen on officials,' said Raymond, as though that explained everything. 'Papi's old friend, M. Lafarge, he just gave me his lot. He did send away to the Bureau but ... when the paperwork came he took one look at it and threw it in the bin. "*Les papiers,*" *il m'a dit,* "*sont inimaginables.*"'

'When will you plant?' I asked him.

'In the summer,' he said, draining his beer. 'Don't worry. We'll leave a few for you.'

The next week flew by but before we left I made a brief trip to the *Mairie*. I wanted, if I could, to find out more about the history of Bel-Air. Not that it is at all a grand house, quite the reverse. I can imagine that at one time it was little more than a barn, with a *cheminée* and sleeping accommodation in the attic. Our Mayor was his usual, friendly self but unable to help. He said that all the records for our commune which, in the last century had seen its population decline from over 2000 to 160 people, were now kept in Agen.

As we had to change trains at Agen for our return flight from Toulouse, we packed up the house early on the last morning. Leaving our luggage in the *consigne automatique* – the numbered lockers on the platform – we set off to see what we could find out in the *Archives Départmentales.*

The public room was crowded. The only person in it not deep into research was a whimpering, wriggling two-year-old. Spectacles were lowered, people sighed, the mild assistant frowned as the young mother re-positioned the child once again on her lap and turned another page. From time to time a senior assistant looked in severely from another room as if trying to judge the exact moment to eject both mother and child. Eventually the pale young girl found what she was looking for, scribbled a few notes and left. The whole room breathed a sigh of relief.

'Now ... exactly what was it we required?' We explained. The gentle forehead lifted and wrinkled.

'It would be very difficult. All documents since the *Revolution ... vous comprenez ...* all the numbers of the sections were changed *mais ... peut-être ... on verra.'* We will see.

Gradually with her considerable help we waded through the crumbling files, the dusty books. We learned, at last, the reference numbers for the house, the barn, the parcels of land. There was much more to do but, it was midday. The Archives would now close until two-thirty. Our train for Toulouse left Agen at 12.55. As we strolled the ten minute walk to the station, we joked about having forty minutes to waste. The joke was on us.

We went to get our luggage, which also contained bread, fruit and cheese for a picnic lunch, and found a large white label stuck right across our locker. *EN PANNE.* OUT OF ORDER. There was no one on the platform. It was, of course, midday. We explained the situation to the swarthy young man behind the ticket window.

'Ah yes,' he said. 'It happens sometimes.' It clearly wasn't his problem.

'But we have to catch the train ... to Toulouse! And after that the plane to London. Our passports, our tickets ... they are all locked inside ...'

He looked more sympathetic. 'Go along the platform to door number two,' he said.

We did. There was no one there. The whole station seemed deserted. We returned.

'He must be at lunch,' said the young man. 'Try door number 3.'

Door number three was nowhere near door number two but when we eventually found it, there was no one there either. By now it was after twelve thirty.

The young man must have telephoned someone for, after another five minutes, which seemed like half an hour, from opposite ends of the platform two officials appeared. The first to reach us peeled off the white label with a flourish and, taking our numbered ticket, punched up the numbers which should have released the catch. '*Ça ne marche pas,*' he glared.

If it was that easy, we thought, we could have done it. The second official closed in. He looked affronted. '*C'était moi!*' he said. 'I put that label on. Someone had put money in the ticket slot. It is definitely out of order!'

Most of the other lockers were empty, their doors hanging open. Why on earth had this someone chosen our locker?

'M. et Mme are going on the train to Toulouse,' said the first official, looking at his watch. We were all looking at our watches.

'We need the machine!'

What now, we worried? What machine?

'*D'accord!* But ... Where is it then?'

The second man clapped his hand to his head and set off down the platform. He reached the far end and disappeared. He came out again, raced towards, then past us, our heads turning to follow him. He ran to the opposite end of the platform where, again, he disappeared from view. By now a small crowd of passengers had collected on the opposite platform where the train for Toulouse was due in less than five minutes. At last the official emerged clutching a square metal box. Panting and red faced he ran towards us. He stopped.

'*J'ai oublié le code!*' he shouted.

He screwed up his face in a supreme effort of concentration, then started towards us again. He pointed his machine at the locker and pressed the numbered keys. Nothing happened. He tried again. The door flew open. We grabbed our luggage and ran down the steps, along the subway, and up the other side as the train pulled in. We fell into our seats, hot, and dishevelled. Weak with relief, we devoured our bread and cheese, regarded all the while with cool amusement by the elegant woman in the opposite seat. *Ah, les Anglais!* was written large upon her exquisitely made-up face.

By the time we returned in July there were many changes. In the orchard there was a brand new hydrant which was fed by water from the river Lot. Plans to pump from the Lot had been in progress for several years but until some reluctant farmers had been persuaded of the benefits, nothing could be done, as the pipes had to cross their land. Now it seemed there was accord.

'If I'd thought it would ever happen,' said Raymond wrily, 'I would never have paid for a new lake five years ago but ...' He shrugged. 'If you get a hose connector to fit the hydrant,' he added, 'you can water your garden when it's not in use.'

This was good news. Mains water in France becomes ever more expensive and the water from the Lot, though, as I discovered, smelling very strongly of river, was a fraction of the cost.

The long buttercup meadow which stretched down from the wood was now a baked, brown desert, spiked with 3100 brand new wooden stakes. They had been hammered into the ground at metre intervals through continuous strips of black plastic which were to discourage the weeds. Raymond explained that weed killer cannot be used for three years on new vines. He and Jean-Michel were now working all day with two-handed augers to make the holes for the vines. He came down to the pool to sit for a moment and have a drink but he was too busy to swim.

'Tomorrow we plant,' he said. 'Merlot and Cabernet Sauvignon.'

He looked exhausted but, before he left, reminded us to come down that evening as *Nabucco* was to be televised live from Orange. It didn't start until 10 p.m. and it was almost one in the morning before it finished. Raymond insisted on staying up but we had to wake him for the best bits.

At nine the next morning we were all in the new vineyard ready to begin. Raymond proudly unloaded and carried out the first tray of vines and showed us exactly how to plant them. Pierre, a young *pâtissier*, temporarily without a job, was helping out and also Claude, another neighbour, who lives in the house where Anaïs's nephew once lived. Often the holes they had made were a little too deep and we had to put in a handful of earth before positioning the plant just so, turning its natural curves from the graft towards the stake. Halfway down the row I put in a vine and felt it move. On taking it out I found the hole already occupied by a huge toad. Raymond scooped it out with a trowel, whereupon it went down the next one. We worked slowly and steadily, Mike going back to the farm with the van again and again for more plants. As I placed the vines, Claude came behind me with a shovel to fill the holes with earth.

A heavy smoker, he had not yet lit up and I noticed that his teeth were unusually white. 'You've given up smoking?' I enquired. He unbuttoned his shirt and showed me the patch on his chest. He grinned.

'C'est un timbre,' he said. It's a stamp. *'On dit ... on est timbré.'*

It was a nicotine patch. *'C'est un secret ... un secret de polichinelle.'* That turned out to be the kind of secret which gets passed from one to the other.

Claude enjoys teaching me idiomatic French. As we progressed down the long row and looked back at the vast size of the operation, he shook his head.

'Ah, Raymond,' he said to me. 'He is still so young in spirit but ... he doesn't seem to realise ... it's the legs that will be the problem!'

I watched Jean-Michel, fit and bronzed after a few days by the sea and, thankfully, there didn't seem to be much wrong with his legs.

At the weekend Philippe came up to inspect the vineyard and seemed impressed. He had been fishing and brought us a bucket of small fish for our supper. They were still alive. 'Just pour the water off a little before you want to cook them,' he said breezily.

During the next week friends and family arrived from all directions. My cousin David came with Tristan, a young man he had met at a conference in America the previous

February, and had invited to spend Easter in London. At the end of March David had developed full-blown Aids and in one of its most frightening forms. He had CMV, cytomegalovirus, which often leads to blindness. He rang America to tell Tristan to cancel his trip but the young man simply said it looked as though he had better come as soon as possible. He gave up his job as a supporter of carers for disabled students and came to care for David. He is still here. David is now very frail and completely blind and without Tristan would be lost.

When they arrived that summer at Toulouse they brought freezer bags full of the chemotherapy which took an hour each morning to feed through a Hickman line into David's chest. Still able to see then, once this was done, he was up and eager to start on the garden. He weeded and cut out all the old rhizomes on my iris bed. We had been given a box of prize irises, and Tristan and Matthew dug out a large new bed, and I was sent down to the farm to shovel up bags of dry manure. Grandma came out of her little house to see what I was doing. As I loaded the sacks into the car she came quietly out with a basket of cucumbers, tomatoes, lemons and eggs.

David sieved all the dry *fumier* and we planted the irises; peach, dark blue, yellow and russet colours, and transplanted some of the white ones which Anaïs had grown. Raymond came by and stayed for a beer.

'Anaïs would have enjoyed these,' he said. 'She loved her irises.'

On Sunday we went out to lunch and came back on the road between Villereal and Castillonnes. The first time Mike and I had driven down this very rural road we had been startled to see what looked like a naked woman, with huge breasts and bright red nipples, bursting out of the top of a small, spreading tree. Not surprisingly we had slowed down. She turned out to be part of a fantastic display of primitive sculpture in the garden of an otherwise perfectly ordinary farm. There was a simple parking sign on the opposite side of the road so, clearly, one was expected to stop and look. We pushed open the gate and wandered into an individual world of fantasy.

The figures were life size, often unashamedly lewd, and there was a feeling of sheer fun about the whole crowded scene. A serpent with a woman's head writhed through the pots of marigolds along the path. In an ancient, tip-tilted cart sat a mannequin wearing a bonnet. The cart was pulled by the front half of a donkey as if coming up from the underworld. A naked man, generously endowed, brandished a spear at another with a devil's face on his bottom. There were figures with two heads, one male, one female, a manic-looking dog about to catch a crow, another woman with wonderful breasts and a real fern growing for her pubic hair. The whole place was guarded by a very old but live swan who lumbered slowly out of his pond towards us.

As we were looking round, a small, silver haired man came bowling in on a tractor. With a mischievous glint in his eye he explained that he was a bachelor and that although he was a farmer he made the figures in the winter when he had nothing much to do. His father had been a taxidermist and he had learned as a boy how to make the wire armatures. 'I make another figure each winter,' he said. 'It keeps me out of mischief and amuses people.'

When we told Raymond about our discovery he laughed.

'He's the brother of the taxidermist that you met when you first came to lunch with us,' he said.

'The one that went home with *une crise de foie* while his wife ate and ate?' I asked. '*Bien sûr!*' said Raymond.

When we took David and Tristan there, the sculptor was in his garden showing some friends around. We spoke about his brother.

'But he's here,' he cried. 'I'll call him out.'

A transformed taxidermist emerged from the house. He

wore pale yellow trousers, a cream silk shirt and two tone shoes. A heavy gold medallion glinted on his chest, and his once greying hair was now a gleaming auburn.

'He's married again,' whispered the sculptor, with a twinkle. He rubbed his thumb and finger together. '*Quelqu'un avec des sous!*'

We wondered whether his brother had divorced the former wife or whether she had simply exploded.

A week later I watched the muck-spreader working in *le grand champ*. As it trundled to and fro, the dried-out field of pale gold stubble was gradually overlaid with swathes of moist brown. There was a strange wet clattering as the shit, literally, hit the fan. The field is so large that a trailer full of muck only covered two rows. In the hot sun they dried slowly to their original tone, turning the whole expanse into a colour chart of browns. Fortunately the wind was in the right direction. By ten thirty it was too hot to garden and I went to the mill to buy *un pain chocolat* for Thomas who had arrived the day before. Had there been any less chocolate I doubt it would have passed the trades description act but – as far as Thomas is concerned – finding the chocolate is half the fun.

Sitting by the pool we were plagued by wasps and soon realised that there must be a nest somewhere. It had been so hot that in spite of our water from the Lot, there were large cracks in the grassed area around the pool. We watched the wasps flying in and out of a particular spot. Raymond advised us to call *les pompiers*. It seemed a bit drastic but squirting insect spray down the hole was ineffective and, eventually, I phoned the fire station.

'We'll come as soon as we can,' said a reassuring voice.

'How much will it cost?' I asked.

'*C'est gratuit, Madame!*'

About seven thirty we received a call.

'Where exactly are you?' We explained.

'Ah yes ... I know where that is. *À bientôt.*'

Thomas gazed longingly down the track hoping for a large red engine complete with 'nee-naw' and a ladder. He was disappointed when it turned out to be a small red van, so old that there was a hole right through the floor under the driver's seat. Two men got out. One was grey-haired and avuncular, the other looked like D'Artagnan – but wore nothing but a gold chain and a pair of swimming trunks. He apologised for his '*torso nu*' of which he was clearly very proud. '*C'est la chaleur, vous comprenez,*' he said, rippling his muscles.

They would soon deal with our little problem. There were not many wasps. However, as they approached the nest across the cracked and dried lawn, an angry crowd flew out. The men turned smartly back to the van and 'grey-hair' donned a protective suit, with gloves and headgear, before he pumped their special anti-wasp liquid into the hole.

'That will fix them,' said D'Artagnan, leaning against the van, arms folded. 'Grey-hair' was not so sure.

'Pour some boiling water down tomorrow, before the sun is up,' he said. 'And just to be quite sure we'll leave you some of our special *produit*. You've got a spray? Good.'

He peeled off his suit. Yes, they would have a drink.

'*Un Ricard?*' 'Grey-hair' brightened. '*Bien sûr!*'

D'Artagnan sadly declined. 'I've already eaten,' he said ruefully, 'but I'd love a beer.'

Raymond had been working in the new vineyard. He came down to join us.

'I know your face,' he said to D'Artagnan.

'Yes, my parents used to live up at ...'

'Ah, of course.'

'Is it true,' he asked Raymond, pointing to us, 'that they've been here every summer for nearly twenty years?'

'*Mais oui.* You didn't know?' Raymond's eyes widened in mock astonishment.

'*Mon Dieu!* We must drop you in a calendar ...'

Raymond smiled knowingly at me. He had already warned me about the calendar. We all smiled knowingly.

'A calendar. What a pleasure. We would look forward to it.'

'How much should we offer?' we asked Raymond as they drove away.

'Well ... you're not here all the year,' he said 'I should think about 100 francs.'

We needed both the boiling water and the rest of their special *produit*, before our wasps were eliminated. When we finally dug up the nest it was much larger than a football.

We are still waiting for the calendar.

David had given us Charles's telescope. We spend so much time marvelling at the night sky at Bel-Air that he thought it the perfect home. Matthew was fascinated and spent hours trying to set it up. The only problem was that there was no handbook and none of us knew anything at all about telescopes. M. Justino in the next village heard of our difficulty. He had a friend, he told us eagerly, a Monsieur Pic, who was a keen astronomer. There was even an *observatoire* on the other side of Fumel. He would take us there. We arranged to meet on the following Friday, but that morning we received a call excusing M. Justino. He was confined to bed with *une crise d'arthrose des vertèbres*. He could not move. Perhaps next week – otherwise, we should just follow the sign to the aerodrome and ask.

We set off with our *lunette astronomique* and drove up into the darkened and unfamiliar hillsides. We hadn't even known there was an aerodrome there let alone an observatory.

At the very top we found a bar, a barbecue, a car park and a crowd of young people just beginning their weekend. Could this really be the place? We enquired about the observatory.

'*Bien sûr,*' said the barman. 'Straight on, 200 metres. You'll see the dome.'

By now it was really dark. We crept slowly along the rough, winding track and just as we thought we were lost, came to a small, square building with an unmistakable dome. A figure stood in the lighted doorway and, as we parked, he came out, pipe in hand.

'*Bonsoir.*'

'*Bonsoir.*'

'*Est-ce que M. Pic est ici?*'

'*Pas ce soir.*'

'Ah ...' We began to explain. He was immediately welcoming. He would be delighted to look at our *lunette*. Another man emerged, younger, round faced, with spectacles and another, older, thin and pale. Very different from our farming friends, they were quiet, serious men. They wore cardigans and had soft hands. Their little club room was sparse but very neat; tools arranged on a board, press cuttings on another, notices of meetings. It had a homely feel. The first man checked our telescope. Yes, it was a good one for a beginner. The lenses, they were excellent. The problem was always one of stability. Tripods were useless.

'This is what you want,' he said. He led us out into the darkness and fixed our telescope to a wooden post which was set in concrete.

'*Voila!*' he said. '*Vous voyez. Rien ne peut bouger.*' He lined it up and focused.

'*Regardez,*' he said to Matthew and there was Jupiter – like a tiny moon with three satellites – and Venus. It was exciting, but there was more to come.

We were invited to climb the wooden staircase up to the dome. We were adjusting to the cramped darkness when, with a great rumbling sound, a section of the dome opened, the sweet night air rushed in and we saw the sky, bursting with stars. They proudly showed us their telescope; a six-sided box like a very long coffin which they had made themselves, and the mirrors which they had ground. Then we took turns to clamber into the confined space to look, first at the galaxy of Hercules – like a spiders web of diamonds, in fact an exploding star which was so far away that no movement was visible – then Jupiter again, much larger. He told us about Mercury and Pluto – the fastest and slowest – the Pleiades and the Pole star.

'It's much better in the winter,' he said. I pictured them snug in their downstairs room in this remote spot, writing their reports and reading their magazines, then putting on scarves and thick woolly hats, climbing the stairs and opening their dome to let in the frosty air and gaze at the stars. These were men with a passion.

By eleven thirty our eyes were tired with looking. We thanked them and paid our 15 francs. *'C'est pas obligatoire,'* they said. 'But now you can come anytime. We are here every Friday.'

We drove home and although it was late we couldn't resist setting up our telescope once more. We marvelled at the craters on the moon and then – how clever we felt – we changed the lens to look again at Jupiter. Venus, alas, had gone to bed. And so did we.

19

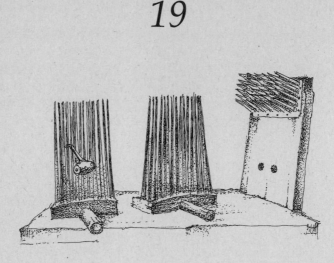

As always that summer, the days flew by. There were hours of frenzied activity; also quiet moments when it was possible just to sit and talk. It is one of my joys that as they grow older both my sons find something special at Bel-Air. It is a place of unwinding. At the end of August Adam cooked a wonderful paella for everyone in celebration of his brother's birthday and, suddenly it seemed, they were all beginning to pack up to leave for England. One morning I could hear Thomas, who was not in the mood for tidying, singing loudly, 'If you're happy and you know it – throw your things on the floor!' Fortunately Caz his mother is wonderfully patient.

A few days later a crestfallen Jean-Michel, who had borrowed our 2CV while his own car was being repaired, came up to tell us that, as he had been coming in from Villeneuve in the early morning, a deer had jumped out in front of him. He had killed it outright. He was as much upset by killing the deer as by the damage done to our car.

'She was full of milk,' he said gloomily. 'What will happen to the young?'

'What did you do?'

He explained that he had been obliged to contact the *Guarde Chasse*. Jean-Michel was well aware that he had no right to take the carcass. We expressed surprise.

'Oh! They might get away with it *dans les Landes,* sometimes,' he said, 'but near Villeneuve … never!' It would be butchered and then … venison would be on the menu at the local old people's home.

I went down to the farm to get some eggs and looked at the 2CV which was standing in the courtyard. In fact there was only a damaged front grill, a bent bumper and a slight dent in the wing which was spattered with blood. Grandma, looking very worried, came out in her slippers.

'*Pauvre Michel,*' she said. '*Il n'a pas le courage de venir la voir.*' I suppose he can't bear to look at it. And she gave me two potato cakes she had just fried. As far as 'pauvre Michel' was concerned, he wasn't at all worried. Jean-Michel would get it fixed. It was as simple as that.

The plum harvest was over for another year. Raymond and Claudette had a few days respite before preparing for the grapes. We had taken them on previous occasions to stay with Spanish friends on the Basque coast. Our friends had now moved inland to Laguardia, a walled town in the wine-growing region of La Rioja, and were constantly asking us when we were coming. Once we had persuaded Raymond and Claudette to come with us we decided not to use the motorway, but to go via Orthez, cross the border at Roncesvalles, and then on down via what Raymond called Pampelune. I found this confusing at first, having never heard this French version of Pamplona before. It was a wonderful journey through, for us, a completely new landscape. We thought we might picnic before we crossed the border but on getting out of the car in the mountains, we were nearly blown away. Once over the other side of the

Pyrénées, it was an altogether balmier world.

We drove into Roncesvalles. Raymond wandered over to what appeared to be a memorial and, wide-eyed, began to recite something about Roland's tomb. Sure enough he was right. I then learned that the Battle of Ronceveaux, as he called it, is part of French legend. It was at this crossing of the Pyrénées in 778 that the most famous of all French heroes, the young count Roland, was killed as he fought a valiant rear guard action to defend Charlemagne against the Basques. Raymond had, as a child, learned verses from the epic poem *La Chanson de Roland* and he clearly found it moving to suddenly find himself on the very spot.

There is also a monastery here, a hostel on the pilgrim's route to Santiago de Compostela. We met a gap-toothed innocent following his own legend who had made the pilgrimage many times. He wore the obligatory cockle shell on his large-brimmed hat and carried a huge knapsack containing a holy picture. He smiled at us, showed us the picture, and explained that that day he had walked from St Jean Pied de Port. Some twenty miles on a mountain road, it was no small achievement. In the church is an effigy of one Sancho VII, called *il Fuerte*, and an amazing, modern window celebrating his victory over the Mameluke. I'm not sure whether he was called Sancho the Proud because of this victory or because he was, apparently, seven feet five inches tall. I was suddenly very conscious of knowing practically nothing about the history of Spain.

Our short holiday was crammed with activity. Our friend Maria is like a Spanish whirlwind. I know no one with more nervous energy, and, of course, with such a limited time for our stay, neither Raymond or Claudette wished to waste a minute. Having just planted his new vineyard Raymond was intensely interested in this great wine-growing area where they had already begun to harvest. José Marie, Maria's husband, took him to visit many bodegas and to talk to the growers. Laguardia itself is like a town on speed. No cars are allowed within the inner walls and people dash about the narrow streets. They are intensely gregarious, greeting each other with slaps on the shoulders and shouts of '*Ola!*' even if they have already met twice that morning. The views from the town are spectacular, perched as it is high up above the vast plain, and the crowds promenade back and forth with proud señoras pushing their prams full of exquisitely dressed children.

It was fiesta time in a nearby small town and, after a meal, off we went. I don't know quite what I was expecting. It was after all a very small, remote town. The sights and sounds which greeted us as we walked down into the square were remarkable. Even in my long ago days of singing in cabaret at the Dorchester or Grosvenor House Hotels, in times when there were such things as big dance bands, I don't ever remember seeing five singers fronting the saxes and trumpets. The music they made was rich and smooth, and the three girls and two men with black, sleek hair wore costumes shimmering with sequins. As the smartly jacketed band played with Spanish bravado, the crowd joined them. They sang all the old Latin American songs. *Amapola*, *La Cucaracha*, *Amor Amor*; it was pure nostalgia. They were very, very good. Only the excellent sound system was modern, worked from a large desk set up in the square.

We were too tired to stay much after midnight but it was a three-day fiesta. The following night – nothing could have kept Raymond away – we arrived to find to our astonishment, an equally flamboyant, but completely different band. There were eight musicians this time and three girl singers in gold trousers who gyrated as they sang.

'These bands must cost a fortune,' I said to Maria. She laughed.

'The village pays,' she said. 'It's quite normal. For fiesta nothing is too good. It is important!'

The square was packed, the atmosphere one of sheer abandon to song and rhythm. This night they were not songs I knew but everyone else sang as they danced, even many of the elderly women, still with such proud backs and erotic movements. A circle of young men turned slowly, clapping and vying to do the most stylish steps.

Suddenly the music stopped. There was a fanfare on the trumpet. Everyone screamed and began to run to the edges of the square.

'What is it?' we asked each other, as we too were pushed into a doorway by the still laughing but very insistent crowd. We had become separated from Maria and, as the shouts went round, '*Il toro del fuego!*' we had no idea what to expect.

There was a sudden hush and into the now-empty square swaggered a tall figure in black, wearing a metal bull's head and shoulders. The crowd roared. As the figure began to paw the ground, from the long, lowered horns, fireworks exploded loudly in all directions. He charged to the far side of the square. Those on our side began to edge out, only to turn for cover, screaming and laughing, as he changed direction and charged towards us. Back and forth he went. Young men would suddenly run out and, sitting down, legs astride, one in front of the other like a boat, would rock and taunt the figure, but as soon as he approached, horns ablaze, they would scramble up and dash into the shelter of the nearest doorway. Young and old clearly enjoyed the real sense of danger, and, as it happened again twice during the evening, we knew what to expect when the trumpet sounded.

Although all the bars were open and serving furiously, there was no sign of drunkeness. The young, especially the young men, were intensely involved, and when they danced they had the kind of skill and energy that one normally associates with professional dancers. It was a real pleasure to watch.

On our last night we went into the town of Logrono. We had a drink at one of the smart bars in the centre of the town and watched the elegant Spanish parading by. Then we spent the rest of the evening sampling the tapas bars in the network of alleys which form the oldest part of town. I don't know whether it was the bechamel balls, the brochettes of pork, the fried quails eggs or the chorizo and chilli: probably the whole combination, all washed down with numerous glasses of *vino tinto*, which made us rather fragile on the return journey, especially the poor chauffeur. Raymond however, was up at the crack of dawn for a last solo walk around Laguardia before leaving.

A few days later I was in Villeneuve. Idly looking up at the statue opposite the tourist office, which I had always thought represented St George killing the dragon, it suddenly struck me that it was not a dragon at all, but an eagle. I went to enquire at the tourist office but, unable to help, they suggested the Archives which were on the next corner. The young woman archivist also wasn't sure. In the meantime, would I like her to photocopy something of the history of the town? Why not. As we talked I glanced down at a large scale map on her desk.

'That's where I live,' I said, locating and pointing to Bel-Air. Her eyes opened very wide.

'*C'est pas vrai*,' she said. I don't believe it.

'Why not?'

She shook her head. '*Mais* ... my great-grandfather was born in that very house,' she said. '*Je m'appelle Sylvie*,' she added, as if that explained everything.

Her great-grandfather, it turned out, was Celestin, Anaïs's young brother-in-law. He had been only sixteen when, in 1889, his older brother Justin had married Anaïs, and brought her to live at Bel-Air.

'*Mais ... votre grandmère ...?*' I was beginning to work it out. Sylvie's grandmother was Madame Esther, Anaïs's

207

niece, whom I had last seen at Philippe's wedding. 'Is she still alive?' I asked.

'*Bien sûr.*'

It was just as well that no one else came in to search through the archives that afternoon. Sylvie was even more passionate about research than I, and considerably more skilled. A few days later she came up to Bel-Air and showed me her detailed files.

I remembered the day, many years before, when her grandmother, Madame Esther, had come up to Bel-Air. She had been very interested to see the house, after such a long time. She was pleased that we had kept much of the original furniture, and that Anaïs's picture hung on the wall. She told me how brave Anaïs had been in her widowhood. She went on to talk about her own great sadness when her only daughter had died of a rapid cancer before she was forty. I had not known that her daughter had been married with two children. Sylvie was the younger.

As I looked at all her research and listened to her story, I realised that for Sylvie, the sudden death of her mother had been disastrously handled. With all her family locked in their inevitable sorrow she had not been encouraged to enquire or even talk about her mother. There had been no space for her to grieve. For a short while she had been sent *en pension* where she was unhappy. Then her father had remarried a widow with children of her own, and although she was kind and tried hard to win the child's affection, Sylvie felt excluded. Perhaps she might have eventually found a certain security there but a few years later her father too had died. She became a very rebellious teenager and it had taken her many years of unhappiness and depression before she could either understand or find herself. The family research was, I imagine, a lifeline.

She ate supper with us and looked all round the house. She took away to photocopy the old documents I had found in the cupboard in the attic, some of which predated the Revolution. When she returned them she, this time, brought her stepmother, with whom she had, at last, found a rapport.

She was a very dynamic, graceful woman, rather like Margot Fonteyn. She talked about the war and about her brother. He had been wounded at Dunkirk, rescued by an English boat and taken back to England but at that time his family knew nothing of this. After a long interval there was still no news, she told us, and they thought he must be dead.

'*Mais* ... the one night that we didn't listen to Radio Londres – there he was!' she said. 'He said "*Je m'appelle Etienne Martigny.*" He then gave his date and place of birth and his regiment and finished with "*Je suis en bonne santé.*" A neighbour heard him – only a lad. He got out his bicycle and tore across the countryside to tell us. He was so out of breath when he arrived,' she laughed, 'he could hardly speak. But ... when he told us ... we all cried.' She wiped her eyes. 'And do you know, he was safe in a camp all that time. He even met your Queen and she shook his hand.'

After they had gone I sat looking again through the hat box in which I had found so many mouse-nibbled treasures. Letters from the First World War, with poignant reminders to those at home to harvest the grapes, or take a cow to market. Letters full of longings, often cruelly dashed, that the terrible war would be over soon, and they would come home. I still have a collection of small almanacs which, with a few exceptions too chewed to be worth keeping, run from 1904 to 1935. They make endlessly fascinating reading. Although they originally cost only ten centimes, the earliest ones have been carefully protected with brown paper covers.

Underneath the calendar for each month, every single day of which bears the name of some saint or other, there is advice for working the land. In April 1904 the reader is urged to sow barley, lentils, flax and hemp, white mustard and rape and lettuces for the pigs. The mention of flax and hemp intrigued me, for Pierre Costes, Anaïs's father-in-law, who was born in 1839, and Bernard, his father before him, both of whom lived at Bel-Air, were both *tisserands* – weavers. In the attic we found some very interesting, crude, and ancient tools which would have been used for carding.

As the years go on, the almanacs are augmented with the occasional poem or sheet of music, and there are illustrations of accordions for sale on almost every other page. There are cures for everything, from gout and asthma, to constipation or a flat chest. There is a lurid advertisement for a cure for drunkeness. It shows a tearful skeleton, with the injunction to 'save the drunkard before alcohol not only destroys his health, his ardour for work and his fortune, but before death makes this very rescue impossible!'

In another advertisement, a certain Doctor Chrestien of Montpelier swears that, in fifty years of practising medicine, he has found nothing more efficacious for the chest than *'pâté and sirop d'escargots.'* The pâté cost one franc, the syrup was double the price. There is no mention of garlic butter.

There are claims for the effects of tisanes made by Trappistes and, in the almanac for 1909, a separate brochure for *'La Tisane Américaine des Shakers'*. Not only tisanes, *les Shakers* also made pills, ointment and poultices, with which they claimed to cure every ailment known to man. One might have expected this brochure to be illustrated with transatlantic images but the French, ever chauvinistic, have placed on each page, between the stories of cures, pictures of such French luminaries as La Fontaine, Madame de Montespan, Molière, and even Louis XV at the age of twenty.

In the almanac for 1909 there is an article about the success of the Paris Metro, which, in its first five years, had expanded from five to thirty-eight kilometres of track. It quotes the unfavourable opinions expressed at the time of the great Exhibition of 1900.

'Not a single Parisien will descend into this molehole.'

'Well they do in London.'

'Huh! What have those Londoners got to lose? In all that fog they might just as well circulate below ground as above! But, I ask you, what Parisian would deprive himself of the view of our splendid trees and boulevards?'

In the review of the year 1906-7, as well as the report of the activities of anarchists in Russia, there is the news that, in London, the proposal to build a tunnel under the channel which frightens so many Englishmen has been abandoned!

In 1909 the decision to impose a collection of personal income tax is adopted by the Chamber of Deputies.

'*Une inquisition intolérable!*' thunders the Almanac for 1910. 'Nothing will escape the clutches of *le fisc!*'

In 1911 they are equally scathing. There is a cartoon of the poor being squeezed in a vice. '*C'est la résurrection de la taille, de cet impôt vexatoire qui fut une des causes de la Révolution!*'

In 1912 and 1913 they are still complaining '*Adieu le secret de vos affaires!*' After that I imagine there were other more pressing problems.

There is a larger Almanac for 1915 which cost 30 centimes. It begins its review from October 1913 in cheerful mood with the reopening, after restoration work, of the Comédie Française. There is a report of the President, M. Poincaré going off on a tour of Spain and one of the marriage in London of Prince Arthur of Connaught.

Gradually, between such snippets as the finding in Florence of the *Mona Lisa,* stolen from the Louvre, the arrests of suffragettes in London, and the cutting of the Panama canal, there are the first rumblings of war. A declaration of accord between France, England and Russia – with a view to maintaining peace – is rudely shattered by the assassination of Archduke Ferdinand and his wife at

Sarajevo. However, this is hardly given more precedence than the shooting of the director of Figaro by Mme Caillaux, wife of the minister of Finance who was, it seems, involved in some controversy at the time. M. Caillaux resigns, Mme Caillaux is arrested and M. Poincaré goes off again, this time to Russia, where he is fêted by the Tsar. Austria gives an ultimatum to Serbia and prepares for war. The whole sorry build-up is quietly but clearly reported, punctuated throughout by the trial of Mme Caillaux who, extraordinarily, having killed the director of Figaro with five bullets, managed to be finally acquitted.

I wonder what Anaïs thought about these events so far away as she worked among her chickens, or drew up her water from the well at Bel-Air. Her husband Justin had finally been absolved from all military duties in 1912 at the age of thirty-six. She could have no premonition of the devastation which the First World War would bring to France, of the decimation of thousands of small villages. Her only son, crippled by polio as a boy, she would have imagined would be safe. But before the war ended even he would be drafted to do menial tasks in the barracks at Montauban.

20

It was Clément's fourth birthday but not, as one might have expected an occasion for jelly and sausage rolls. With his napkin tied round his neck he tucked into a lunch of *foie gras* followed by asparagus, roast veal, cepes, and pommes frites, all of it especially appreciated by the adults. We drank a 1983 Chateau Neuf du Pape with the veal, and champagne with the cake. He did, however, have candles. He also had a new pair of trainers which lit up at the back when he stamped hard. We left him bouncing round the courtyard followed by an already walking Océane, and went back up to the house for a short siesta before getting on with the garden.

We had been late arriving this spring as I had been involved in a new musical for the Covent Garden Festival. We had come by rail, eager to try out Eurostar to Paris, which was better than we had imagined. With not so much as a glimpse of the channel, it was almost impossible to believe that the *Gare du Nord* was not somewhere at the far end of the Northern Line. The TGV from Paris to Agen was less of a pleasure as, without warning, SNCF had booked us into something called the kiosk. We had what must have been the worst seats in the train, facing sideways, with no view. We took refuge in the buffet car for most of the journey, made a note never to repeat the experience and complained bitterly on returning to London.

It was the last week of May. In the already strong early morning sunlight, we picked wild strawberries for breakfast just outside our own porch. The *boule de neige* was past its best but I had never known the garden so fragrant. The syringa, the roses and the honeysuckle in full flower, provided instant aromatherapy each time I rounded the corner. There were fourteen of Anaïs's lilies just about to burst into bloom and the last irises were unfolding. Claudette came up the next morning with a basket of eggs and half a dozen of her large sweet onions. There was the drone of distant tractors as those who had cut their hay were busy turning it. Raymond was undecided and phoned the metereological service at Agen daily. The promised shower for the following night did not materialise.

'I need a shower now, before I cut it,' grumbled Raymond. 'Not afterwards.'

The next day there was a fine misty rain and Claudette and I went to market. It really was *le temps des cerises.* The stalls were heaped with fat, dark, shining cherries – *les Bigarreaux* – the flesh so taut that the staining juice spurted out at the first bite. Claudette bought six chicks at 3F each. The young man put them into a shoebox and punched a couple of holes through which they cheeped incessantly all the way home. She intended to smuggle them under a hen who was already sitting.

'Will it work?' I asked.

'It usually does,' she said. 'But – if she doesn't accept them ...' she shrugged, 'she'll kill them.' Nature red in beak and claw!

When we got home Grandpa was cutting asparagus. With a special tool, rather like a long handled shoe-horn, he walked along the rows looking for those shoots which were just showing their tips.

'*C'est presque finit l'asperge,*' he said, straightening up, hand in the small of his back. '*Premier Avril, jusqu à mi-juin.*'

This is obviously one of the jobs he still lays his claim to, although it entails a great deal of bending and stretching, and a bucket full of asparagus is no light weight. Grandma was still sitting in the courtyard busily cutting up lengths of blue plastic netting. '*C'est pour l'arrosage,*' she said when I enquired.

Jean-Michel was to set up a watering system between the plum trees. The netting, Grandma told me, was to protect the sections of the hose which lie flat on the ground from being eaten by rabbits. Having only ever seen one rabbit in all my time at Bel-Air, apart from the corpse brought in by the wild cat, I was surprised.

She smiled. '*Ah ... qu'est-ce que vous voulez?* If that's what they want, I can do it. I've worked all my life. I can't just sit here now with my hands folded in my lap.'

The hay was cut and all the next evening Raymond worked, turning the swathes in the fading sunlight. The smell was wonderful, the sky a water colourist's dream. Later we went down to the farm and sat outside in the still air. Claudette was trying to put Océane to bed. Her parents were off to visit friends and had left her with her Grandma. Raymond and Grandpa were arguing about the right time to sulphate the vines.

'If you don't do it soon,' roared Grandpa, 'the flowers will open. The pulverisor will scatter the pollen and – *je vous le dis* – they won't fertilise!'

'*Mais,*' said Raymond, 'They don't flower *au même moment – le Merlot et le Cabernet – que c'est difficile!*'

Océane also was being *difficile*. Defeated, Claudette brought her out in her pyjamas. She gave us all a beaming smile and sat happily gnawing on a piece of *confit de canard* – preserved duck – a novel teething aid!

By the end of a fortnight, our garden was beginning to look as though someone cared for it. I had planted cosmos and vervain and the mallows were all coming into magnificent flower. I sat by the pool on our last evening. The blue sky, rosy toward the west, was streaked with strips of grey edged with silver. The newest shoots on the pine trees stretched up into space, the few cones silhouetted against the sky. Apart from the occasional car passing on the road far below, the only moving object in view was a neighbour's water cannon. It spurted in distant silent rhythm until, its ever widening arc reaching its limit, it turned the other way.

At the beginning of July, my second grandson, little baby no-name, was born and, before we left for France, was finally called Elliot James. The weather was perfect when we arrived, with cloudless skies and a light breeze. A monster liquorice reel on a scarlet-wheeled trolley was winding in slowly through the tall maize towards the house and the sound of drenching cooled the air, for Raymond too now had a water cannon. A great swathe had been cut through the rows of maize but it was explained that that would be more than made up for by the increased yield.

Later that evening we had almost finished unpacking when there was the continuous urgent sound of a hooter and an advancing tractor. We hurried out but found Raymond laughing as he thumped the tractor and the noise stopped.

'Don't worry,' he called *'mon klaxon s'est mis en marche.'* It just started by itself, I don't know why. It gave me a fright too.' He sat on the porch to wait for the water cannon to finish winding itself in and reach the top of the row, and fell asleep.

I stood directly behind the machine, the only spot which remains dry, and watched the great lance of water. The jet is interrupted by a metal bracket, which lifts intermittently, forcing some of the water to spray out on the maize close by. I was pleased to see that part of my garden was also benefiting. The next day Mike enjoyed himself driving the tractor, pulling a new trailer like a double length open-topped metal coffin, another of Jean-Michel's devices. It carried the heavy pipes from one field to another to connect from the various hydrants which brought the water from the Lot.

My greengage tree was loaded with fruit. I picked and ate some every time I passed. Claudette's tree at the far end of the orchard appeared to be bare. When I commiserated she laughed. Apparently it had been so heavily laden that a few days before our arrival they had paid a neighbour's children to pick them and take them to the commercial, wholesale market. There were 300 kilos. 'We got 4F a kilo', said Claudette. 'But,' she shrugged and smiled, 'if we'd waited a week we would have got 5F.'

There was wildlife everywhere. Raymond caught a *fouine*, a stone martin, in the trap he puts down for *les ragondins*, the coypus, who are on the increase in our area, doing much damage to both crops and the banks of ponds. I saw a large *ragondin* with its thick, sleek, rump lolloping along our track. The traps they use do not wound the animal. They are long, open-ended cages with a floor in the centre which pivots, causing both end doors to fall shut. In the house there was a preying mantis on the draining board and a tree frog sitting behind the kitchen scales but the worst problem that spring was mice in the cupboard.

We had unwisely left a few nuts in what I had imagined to be a stout plastic box. They had chewed a hole through a corner of the floor of Anaïs's ancient cupboard and had rampaged over everything. The cupboard emptied, scrubbed and repaired and all the contents washed, we did not want a repeat performance. Where had they come in? One intrepid visitor gave us the clue and we removed the heavy fireback to find a positive mouse's highway winding up to a hole in the wall, wide and deep enough for a regiment. It took a great many stones to fill it and we hoped that they would find the cement more of a problem than plastic and wood.

I spent a day sitting with Grandma shelling *les cocos* for bottling. These are especially delicious white beans, rounder and fatter than normal haricots. You cannot buy them commercially preserved because they tend to disintegrate. If the pods are beginning to dry it is a simple chore, otherwise it becomes tedious. But they are superb cooked in a rich tomato sauce with garlic and basil. We always take some back to London. Grandma was pleased to have another task. Her eyesight is no longer good enough to read very much, or to knit. She finds it very hard to adjust to increasing incapacity and is always worried that she is not pulling her weight with the innumerable tasks on the farm.

The weather grew even hotter. We spent a great deal of time in the pool and wondered how we had ever managed without one, and Raymond was thankful that this was the year he had managed to buy his water cannon. There were so many around spraying water in every direction that I began to think that the river Lot must eventually dry up. However, when we next crossed it at Villeneuve for the Saturday market, it looked as deep and dark as always.

During the evening there was a fierce wind from the south-west which hurled over the sun umbrellas and then vanished as suddenly as it had arrived. It seemed to gather strength and returned bearing ominous clouds, this time from the south-east. We cancelled plans to eat our trout, barbecued with garlic and rosemary, by the pool and retreated to the porch. We had hardly finished when the heavens opened. It was still raining when we went to bed at 10.30 and still raining at midnight when I put out the light. And all night long the water cannon wound slowly up towards the house. It didn't understand that it was raining. Senselessly efficient, the little spring tightened, the ratchet turned at measured speed and the lance of water got ever nearer. One might surely have imagined that this mechanical miracle might actually have been fitted with a rain measuring device. Just a simple gauge which, when it reached a reasonable number of centimetres, might have paused in its labours and, like the rest of us, thanked God for the sweetest things of all, a night of heavy rain, followed by a brilliantly sunny morning.

On Sunday we celebrated Raymond's sixtieth birthday. Raymond, who usually adores parties, was strangely reluctant, but Claudette and his children insisted. Like most people whose work is largely dependent on their physical strength, he fears old age. He went quietly about his tasks while a hall was hired, menus were arranged and *Bonne Retraite* was written on the cake and on a banner to be tied across the far end of the room. Some sixty of us assembled at midday outside the *Salle Municipal* at Condat which has a shady garden with a stream running down to the Lot some yards away. The food was good, the service abominably slow, but the conversation animated.

As usual, it was *les beaux jours d'autrefois* that they talked about. As they reminisced, a nephew complained, fortunately out of earshot of Raymond, that it was *les agriculteurs* who had killed the countryside. '*Plus de gibier, plus, d'oiseaux,*' he lamented – no game or birds left. Concern about wildlife? A somewhat unusual sentiment I thought until I learned that he belonged to a club *des Gourmands*.

Philippe's mother-in-law remembered how she and her friends would walk to school. Her eyes shone as she told of the long climb up to the village. 'It took us half an hour to get to the top,' she said. 'Then we would take off our boots and put on proper shoes. How cold they felt – but our feet were warm from walking. But it was coming home that was wonderful; the flowers that we would pick, the fruit in season, and so many fascinating creatures. It always took us over an hour, although it was downhill, because there was so much to interest us. What do the children know of the countryside now?' she asked. The others agreed, nodding sadly.

I wondered what they would think of the lot of city children now who are driven to school and posted fearfully in through the doors; children who never have the chance to meet strangers, or to form judgements of their own. I marvel at my own childhood when I would often sit on a gate talking to strange people who came walking by from the workhouse, a mile or so down the road. Old sailors who would tell me tales and occasionally, batty old women with bundles. Sometimes they would knock on our front door for boiling water to wet the pinch of tea they had been given. Often my mother would cut them a slice of cake. We talked to them and made up our own minds and I don't ever remember feeling threatened. It gave me a sense of confidence and when, as a child, I did meet potential trouble, a priest as it happens, I was quickly able to avoid it.

For Raymond's special celebration, after the salad with gambas, the *galantine de volaille*, and, of course, a *rôti de boeuf*; the cake was carried in and we sang 'Happy Birthday' in French and then in English. Raymond made a touching speech. Clément blew out the candles which had to be re-lit and Océane put her finger in the cream icing, but everyone had a great time. I have a fond memory of Raymond and Claudette whizzing round the room to, of all things, 'The Boogie Woogie Bugle Boy of Company B'.

Les Fostaires arrived and we took them down to Laguardia. We were too early for fiesta but had our usual whirlwind few days. Maria took us up to a mountain village to buy chorizo, the local spicy sausage. They had just been made and were hanging in bright and aromatic festoons. About twenty old ladies were crammed in the next tiny room playing cards, with yet more coming across the square, carrying chairs to join them. On the way home we came through a village where they were about to close the square for the running of the young bulls. The only problem was the one car still parked in the middle. There were constant and ever angrier injunctions from the loudspeaker but when the owner finally arrived it was immediately apparent what he had been doing in the interim. He was so drunk that finding the car was difficult enough, fitting the key in the door was impossible. A friend helped him and got in, intending to drive. The car owner would have none of it. Disgusted, the friend got out to remonstrate. That was a mistake. The owner got in, seized the wheel and the car raced around the square. It was more exciting than the eventual running of the bulls, and a great deal more dangerous.

We visited one of the oldest bodegas – Marques de Riscal – and saw thousands of bottles covered, not only in dust and cobwebs, but mould. I saw one bottled in 1912 for the XVIII *exposition du vin* at Bordeaux. Surprisingly, these vintage wines are re-corked every twenty to twenty-five years, in one swift, in and out movement.

'If they are not worth the trouble it is instantly obvious,' said the guide, wrinkling his fine nose. We visited the thirteenth-century monastery at Najera with its five towers, a choir stall of exceptional beauty, and a Virgin in a grotto saturated with the perfume of bunches of lilies. Spain always seems so extreme and exotic.

We left next morning very early and drove back to Monflanquin where the square was full of nothing more dangerous than inches of straw and chicken feathers scattered beneath the long wooden tables for another medieval banquet that evening.

Although it said 8.30 on the ticket we were not even allowed to take our places until after 9 p.m. We then enjoyed over an hour's entertainment in the square while, backstage, the hundred ducks set up on two long spits behind the church refused to cook. The strong wind was blowing the heat the wrong way and on the part of the chefs there was much shaking of heads and scurrying about. We, the revellers, most of whom had made some attempt at medieval costume, some quite splendid, were perfectly content. We enjoyed the usual young musicians with their authentic instruments and songs and they were followed this year by a curious, surreal cabaret.

Into the square came a girl with white face, arms and legs. Dressed in pale rags, her silver hair was oddly shaved. Behind her she pulled a delicate metal cart on which were a curved brass horn, a bunch of faded flowers and lengths of pale gauze. Although there was a taped sound-track, it did not seem incongruous, consisting as it did of irregular percussion and a keening sound which was strange enough to fit into any period. After a few moments, during which she had everyone mesmerized by her odd, slow, movements, her head tilted as though listening to some enchanted music only she could hear, another figure bounded in. It wore a grey, shaggy costume, like rag rugs, and an animal mask, and it travelled on all fours, holding in its hands short, cloth-covered, wooden stilts, like hooves. There followed a weird kind of ballet which had the crowd, including a great many previously noisy children, completely enthralled.

Eventually the 'beast' was tamed and unmasked to reveal a handsome young man and they hauled off their cart to great applause. They were followed by the Romanian musicians, by now familiar visitors.

All the food was prepared by a team of farmers' wives, and was very good. We ate *terrine de volaille, tarte au saumon et aux épinards*, which was especially delicious, and

222

eventually, just before midnight, the ducks, cooked at last. There was as much local wine as you could drink and great bowls of fruit salad to finish. Raymond and Claudette, happily not babysitting, enjoyed it too.

A few days later it was Claudette's birthday. Raymond came to make sure that we would all go down after supper. He had bought her something special this year.

What was it? He would not tell us, but 'I know what she'll say,' he grinned, '"*Encore du travail!*" More work!'

Eventually he could keep it a secret no longer. He was about to go with Jean-Michel to collect two peacocks. By nine thirty we had all given our presents and were waiting to cut the cake. Véronique handed her a small box which she unwrapped. It contained a tin of maize grains.

'What is it for?' asked Clément, echoed as always by Océane. Claudette looked perplexed. 'Perhaps it's to make *le pop corn*,' she said.

She was genuinely astonished when, out of the darkness, came Raymond and Jean-Michel carrying a pair of handsome peacocks, their feet loosely tied with string. The birds regarded us all with an untroubled stare. '*Oh là! Oh là là là!*' she exclaimed. She stroked them with her practised hand and talked to them in the high, singsong voice she uses to all her animals. She was clearly thrilled. At last she cut the cake, Raymond poured the wine and we all sang 'Happy Birthday'. Clément and Océane amused themselves cleaning all the plastic chairs with two little dish cloths and a bowl of soapy water, and the peacocks gazed round at their new home.

They did indeed make her more work. For the first few weeks they lived with the rest of the birds. At night they slept high up in the chicken barn. But by day they roamed far and wide and she was always having to search for them in the evening. This year Jean-Michel, ever practical, has solved the problem by making them a very large aviary the length of a barn. Claudette hopes they will breed and then she will be able to train the young birds to stay fairly close to the house. I hear their strange cry up at Bel-Air and think of the General's wife in Anouilh's *Waltz of the Toreadors* eternally calling her husband, 'Léon, Léon!'

Before *les Fostaires* left they wanted to take us out to eat at our gastronomic find, the Hotel de Quercy at Lauzerte. It was a very hot day and we were surprised to find even the lower streets of the town crammed with both vans and people until we learned that it was the 54th year of the Dog Fair. M. Bacou, the chef's father, who often takes the orders, was apparently already at the fair. Madame welcomed us and there was a great air of bustle as the last diners arrived and took their places in the pleasant room, the half-closed shutters shielding us from the heat outside. They were mostly family groups with children perched on cushions, and grandmothers adjusting their spectacles to read the menu.

We chose from the 165F menu, the most expensive, apart from a menu surprise at 225F. We wanted the pleasure of deciding for ourselves, but it was not easy, with such a choice.

'Perhaps you would like ... just a little soup, while you decide?' suggested Madame. We sipped away and made our final order. We chose as many different dishes as possible as we knew we would inevitably taste from each other's plates. For the first course we had *foie gras* either cold or hot. The cold was served with both red and black currants and a sprig of mint. Raymond would not have approved! The hot version was fried quickly with apples which had been cooked in honey and spices. They were both delicious, but I think I prefer it cold. Next we had a choice between *ris de veau, saumon, or sandre* – a river fish with thick, firm flesh and a delicate flavour. Judith chose the sweetbreads – the *timbale de ris de veau aux cèpes et champignons* – and it looked so beautiful when it arrived in a white china goblet with a pastry lid. The *sandre* was arranged with the thinnest of sliced potatoes and a sauce of sorrel and red wine; and the salmon, in a wonderful hollandaise sauce with almonds, was sandwiched in filo pastry and served with *oignons confits* which I have never tasted before. They were deep red, almost caramelized and delicious.

There was much passing of plates. 'You must just taste this – it's so good!' There were sighs and groans of pleasure and licking of fingers. We drank a Gaillac Blanc Sec which was perfect, and as we wiped up the last smear of sauce and waited for our next course we watched a father at an adjoining table carefully cutting up steak for his small son. The child, napkin tied firmly round his neck, became impatient and slid off his chair. There was a sudden great noise of barking just outside and the child quickly remounted. There were raised voices and Madame came in with a flushed face and disapproving look.

'*Les chiens!*' she said. 'And – as if we would have a table at this hour!'

Was our food to our taste, she asked. At our enthusiastic replies she smiled. 'Ah well, we have the chef you see.' She served our red wine, a Cahors, her good humour restored.

Next we ate a *filet mignon de veau* cooked with truffles and served with a little mound of finely chopped egg and mushroom. Barry chose a tournedos with a small slice of *foie gras* on the top and served with a square of layered courgettes and tomatoes. It was all beautifully presented, carefully cooked and just the right amount. We nibbled from a very good cheeseboard and then came the difficult task of choosing a desert from a long list which included mousse of mango and passion fruit, chocolate, or raspberry; tart with apricot or spicy fruits; and various ice creams. Barry was pleased to find *Tarte Tatin*, made this time with pears instead of apples and Madame apologised that they had completely run out of *crème fouettée*.

As we drank our strong black coffee with a square of bitter chocolate we delighted in the growing success of this unpretentious restaurant and wondered whether Frederic Bacou, the young chef, would, in the end, be persuaded to try his skills in grander surroundings. His mother had already told us that hoteliers from Switzerland had already tried to lure him away.

'Only once *Maman*,' he protested. 'They rang again, twice,' she insisted proudly.

This was their fifth year at the Hotel de Quercy. Frederic did his training first at Toulouse and then spent two years at Mazamet, returning to Toulouse for a further year to study wine under *'un professeur ... qui m'avait passionné.'* He had worked all over the south-west, and finished with a season in Lorraine. On his return from a holiday in Paris, his parents had told him that the Hotel de Quercy, then extremely run down, and without any gastronomic reputation at all, was for sale.

'That same afternoon I went to look at it and to talk to *le patron*,' he said, his eyes still alight with the excitement of it all. 'Within three months we had begun our project. If it isn't a success, it's not the end of the world, but I wanted to try. It's always been my ambition. I have worked in really grand places, but I'm not cut out for that style of thing ... It is very hard. I want to run a restaurant with a *cuisine ... comme on l'a fait nous ... c'est beaucoup plus sincère.* I want a place with *un atmosphère chaleureuse* where one can eat and drink really well and still be at ease.'

He has certainly created just that, and, as far as we are concerned, long may he continue to do so.

21

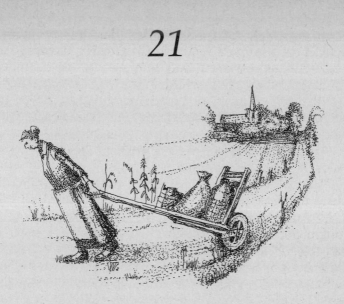

Les Fostaires left for England and the weather stayed fine for the next two weeks. We went to Toulouse to collect my cousin David, very frail now and needing a wheelchair, but still determined to come for what we feared must be his last visit. Tristan could not accompany him because his passport had been suspended in some battle with the Home Office. If he left England he would not be allowed to re-enter. David spent much of his time resting but still kept an eagle eye on the garden. In the cool of the evening he walked slowly up to the new vineyard. He was pleased to see that all the plants looked sturdy, some already bearing their very first grapes. We went out to lunch almost every day, to all his favourite places; Bonaguil, Monpazier and Villeneuve-sur-Lot. One afternoon he was very tired and unwell. He quietly disappeared and slept for many hours then, as the sun began to slant lower through the trees, he suddenly appeared with his Missal and his glasses. It was a beautiful evening, still and warm, the sky intensely blue.

He stood for a moment looking down across the great field to the distant valley.

'Would you like me to celebrate a Eucharist?' he asked. He had never done this before. A little unsure, we fetched as instructed a glass of wine and three small pieces of bread on a saucer. We each read a lesson. David spoke the familiar words in a strong, clear voice that earlier had been faint and breathless and this simple act, without the normal trappings, became at once vivid and unforgettable.

There was such a magnificent harvest of plums this year, due in part to the new watering between the trees, the system put in place by Jean-Michel, and protected from invisible rabbits by Grandma. The branches hung low with the weight of fruit. There were just so many plums that, although officially retired from harvesting them since the arrival of Jean-Michel, Mike and I joined all hands to clear the ground before the giant umbrella could be unfurled. A lavender carpet under the rows of small trees, the plums were so large they looked like heaps of violet eggs laid by some great exotic bird. We were to harvest over 120 tons of plums that summer – 240000lbs of fruit, which, when dried, would become 30000 kilos of prunes. It is Raymond's principal source of income and not one plum is left. The last, and most neck-aching job of all, is the tapping of each last plum off the tree with a very long bamboo cane. Raymond and Claudette were clearly delighted with this year's crop, the best ever. But, like all farmers, as though reluctant to tempt providence, they hastily compared it with other disastrous harvests when very late frosts had decimated the yield.

At the end of the week they came up for lunch. I made a creamy soup with carrots and lentils and an *hors-d'oeuvre* with avocados and tuna, bottled by our Spanish friends. Then we ate chilli con carne which Grandpa had in fact ordered, but although I had made it half strength, he still found it just a little too hot.

'*C'est très bon,*' he said, wiping his face. '*Mais ... c'est un peu trop fort!*'

After salad we ate ice-cream and a totally out of season Xmas pudding which I had saved.

'*Ah le pudding de Noël!*' they all exclaimed. They are really getting the taste for it, and think it a great pity to only eat it once a year.

We got out the old wedding photographs of 1933 which I had been lent. There is nothing that starts such a chain of reminiscing. Grandpa put on his spectacles and Raymond borrowed Mike's, the better to peer at the rows of wedding guests of long ago.

'*Oh là! C'est le Père Laurence.*'

'*Non!*'

'*Si! Regarde. C'est le même visage.*'

'*C'est bizarre.* You have to jump a generation. How like his son he looks!'

'*Petit à petit* ... you can sort them all out.'

'That was Madame Delbert. She was always complaining. A pain here – a problem there.'

Grandpa laughed. 'You know what they say.'

Raymond grinned. '*Celui qui se plaint tout le temps – c'est celui qui vit le plus longtemps.* Those who complain the most – live the longest.' And Grandpa capped it by saying it in Occitan.

'*Lou che fai touzor piou piou. A cho lou che mai biou.*'

They identified Madame Esther, Sylvie's grandmother, and her great grandmother, *la couturière.* She wore a dark dress much decorated with delicate white piping, no doubt to advertise her expertise. Both she and her daughter were apparently wonderful gossips.

'Anyone who went to the dressmakers,' said Grandma with a smile, 'would soon know all the news of the region.'

They began talking about the various plots of land owned by the wedding guests. Some were fertile, some less so. That reminded Raymond of a relative who had 'une petite prairie' which was adjacent, not to his own house, but to that of a neighbour. Although the hay was regularly cut and baled he never declared it and was piqued to find that one year he received a demand for tax for cultivated land. Off he went to Perigueux to plead his case with the Inspector, who said 'I'd better come and see for myself.'

'Sûrement!' agreed Lucien, 'Whenever you wish, but ... you'd better leave it till the end of July because ... I have to take my wife away for a cure.'

Unfortunately someone, the neighbour perhaps, had already sent to Perigueux a photograph of Raymond bailing the hay the previous year. Lucien was alarmed when he had a sudden call from the local Inspector announcing that the departmental Inspector was in the region and would be calling on him in an hour or two.

'Pas de problème,' lied Lucien, who then telephoned Raymond to come and get the rest of the hay – immédiatement!

All was not lost however. The prairie was some way up the hill, the house at the bottom. The Inspector arrived. Yes, he would be glad to try a glass of something special. To Lucien's delight he turned out to be a fellow Rugby enthusiast.

Raymond chuckled as he remembered how he had collected up the last few bales while the two men had discussed every Rugby match within living memory, drinking a glass between each one. At last the Inspector had looked at his watch, cried 'Mon Dieu! Is that the time. I must fly!' and had disappeared.

A few days later I had an unexpected visitor. Mme Ducrois brought her sister to visit Bel-Air. I had met Mme Ducrois at Véronique's wedding. She had been very interested to hear where we lived. She remembered cycling up to Bel-Air with her sister, when they were young girls.

'I'd love to bring her to see you one day,' she had said. 'She lives in Paris but comes for the holidays.' I had assured her of a welcome but by now I had quite forgotten about it.

The two elderly ladies were delighted to relive their girlhood. They chattered non-stop as they recognised familiar landmarks. They had grown up in the family home, a grand house about two miles away, now only used in the holidays. During the war they had been sent on their bicycles to buy eggs and rabbits from Anaïs, who by then was in her seventies.

'This is where she kept the eggs in a wooden box ... in here,' said Mme Ducrois.

'Goodness, how pretty you've made it.'

'That's right,' said her sister. 'This was her room. It was filled with bits and pieces. We were a bit scared of her,' she giggled.

'*Oh ... elle était gentille mais ...* she seemed so very old to us.' This made them both burst out laughing.

'She spoke a lot of patois ... sometimes we didn't understand her, did we? And those awful rabbits!'

'*Ils étaient terribles,*' cried Mme Ducrois. 'I think they must have been semi-wild – or perhaps a special breed – but they had huge claws. We had to carry them home in our bag on the handlebars. Anaïs would tie their legs but they wriggled about. Didn't they scratch our knees as we rode along!'

'We loved to come up here,' said her sister. 'It was an adventure, but we hated bringing home those awful rabbits.'

They too looked at the old wedding groups with great nostalgia. Old photographs are very powerful and unlock many memories.

So many people remember Anaïs, although she died in 1963. They often talk about her coming down with her wooden wheelbarrow to carry her frugal shopping from the village. She then had to pull it back up the drive to

Raymond's farm, take the winding path around his first meadow, go through the wood and up along the edge of *le grand champ* to the pond. It is uphill all the way to Bel-Air. Occasionally her well ran dry and she would bring down a large container to get water from a spring outside the village. She would love to gossip, but would not stay long, in case her son complained.

She would invite Mme Vidal the shopkeeper's wife to bring her small children up to catch frogs in the pond.

'They had a lovely time,' smiled Mme Vidal. 'She was very kind. She gave me cuttings of her hydrangea. The one I then gave you cuttings from. You remember? *Eh oui.* The plants live longer than us.'

Anaïs's son Aloïs was apparently jealous and, after the children had caught two or three frogs, he would beat the water with a stick to frighten them away, saying 'That's enough.'

The children would then tie one of the frogs they had already caught to their lines and jig it up and down calling, 'Look Aloïs, here's another!' to tease him.

In 1955 the village at last installed a communal stone washing trough with running water. Anaïs was then eighty-four. She came down to the shop and stood in wonder at this modern phenomenon. Then, to everyone's amusement, she grabbed a piece of someone else's washing and scrubbed away for the sheer pleasure of it, saying, 'Oh if only I had something like this up at Bel-Air.' What would she make of my washing machine?

In three weeks time we shall be leaving London once more as we have done for the past twenty years to spend our summer at Bel-Air. Our children and grandchildren will join us in August. Already there are piles of books, packets of tea and jars of marmalade collecting in odd places. There are notes pinned up, instructions for those of the family who come to stay in the London house. I feel restless and slightly disoriented as if I am already half-way between one home and another. I know that the last week will telescope into a mad scramble of unfinished business but that when the car is finally loaded and we leave I shall feel a great sense of freedom.

We bought a long-derelict house which I like to feel was just waiting for us to arrive. With the changes which we have inevitably made we have still tried to keep its original style. Apart from the creation of a bathroom where there was once a staircase, we have made no structural alterations. When we go in the spring we have an annual debate about whether to add a window in the main room. When we return in high summer we remember why we shouldn't. The shade and cool are then precious. The pool, which at first seemed so alien, has begun to blend into the garden and has given us all hours of pleasure.

We have had the great good fortune to have wonderfully kind neighbours, to be accepted into a community whose way of life we knew little about. We have learned a great deal. And there is still so much to learn.

I recently discovered the house where Anaïs was born in 1871. I have her school books which are endlessly fascinating, and I wonder where she went to school. Many children at that time had no schooling. It was not until the 1880s that state education for all was introduced – *gratuite, obligatoire, laïque* – free, compulsory and secular. I suspect Anaïs may well have been educated in a school maintained by a religious community. I have the promise of a chat with an eighty-three-year-old belle-mère who comes in the summer and will, I am assured, remember all she knows of local history. She is a Protestant and they have, I learn, a very strong oral tradition.

There is the ongoing research into the history of Bel-Air itself. With Sylvie's help we have established that one François Costes, who was born elsewhere in 1758, once lived there; but there is much more to do. The latest discovery that there was once a church, St Nicholas, between us and the village, has us all excited. Raymond fancies a large ring of trees in the middle of a neighbour's field as the original location but, until the sunflowers are harvested, we can't investigate to see if the foundations are still there.

After the Revolution many churches were destroyed and the stones carted away and used to build houses and barns. Who knows, perhaps part of Bel-Air was built with consecrated stones? Our earliest and originally, I suspect, the only window, has a hand-cut stone arch and transom. There were once two wooden shutters studded with nails. Only one remains, the other having been long ago replaced with glass. Sometimes as I look around in the evening, I long for one of those cinematic transformations. How I would love to see Bel-Air dissolving from one shot to another, travelling back in time to show the very first people who stood in that peaceful spot, halfway down the long slope of the land, and decided to build a house.

In a few weeks time we shall finally turn up the track by the side of the orchard. As we catch our first glimpse of our wide and welcoming porch decorated with flowers by our neighbour and good friend, we shall once again be very thankful that they did.